# Cryptocurrency

## – 2 Books in 1

*Everything You Need to Know to Take Advantage of the 2021 Bitcoin Bull Run!*

damages that may befall them after undertaking information described herein.

Additionally, the information in the following pages is intended only for informational purposes and should thus be thought of as universal. As befitting its nature, it is presented without assurance regarding its prolonged validity or interim quality. Trademarks that are mentioned are done without written consent and can in no way be considered an endorsement from the trademark holder.

# Bitcoin and Ethereum

*Learn the Secrets to the 2 Biggest and Most Important Cryptocurrency – Discover how the Blockchain Technology is Forever Changing the World of Finance*

damages that may befall them after undertaking information described herein.

Additionally, the information in the following pages is intended only for informational purposes and should thus be thought of as universal. As befitting its nature, it is presented without assurance regarding its prolonged validity or interim quality. Trademarks that are mentioned are done without written consent and can in no way be considered an endorsement from the trademark holder.

# Table of Contents

# Introduction

Bitcoin has taken the world by storm once again when it crossed $20,000 per BTC in December of last year. After more than 2 years of bear market, the most famous cryptocurrency surpassed its previous all time high.

A lot of people are now trying to improvise themselves as professional investors and are losing a lot of money, only helping those who actually know what they are doing accumulate an incredible amount of wealth that will lead to generational fortunes.

To join the club of the few investors that actually make it, you need the right knowledge and the right mindset. Notice how we did not include a large initial capital. In fact, while having more money to invest means having more fire power, it is not necessary to have thousands of dollars to accumulate cryptocurrency and build wealth.

In fact, when we started investing in cryptocurrency we only had a few hundreds to put into the market, but that sum yielded us thousands and thousands of dollars over the span of a few years.

In this book you are going to discover everything there is to know about the fascinating world of cryptocurrency. From the operation of the Bitcoin blockchain to more advanced projects, like Uniswap and Compound.

If you diligently study the content of this book, we are sure you are going to see take your crypto knowledge to the next level. This also means you are going to see amazing results in a relative short period of time, since this bull run is offering an amazing number of opportunities.

To your success!

*Kevin Anderson*

# Chapter 1 - The History of Bitcoin

First of all, who created Bitcoin?

Nobody knows! The creator of Bitcoin used the pseudonym Satoshi Nakamoto, but we know nothing about his identity. Satoshi could be a person or group of developers anywhere in the world. The name is of Japanese origin, but Satoshi's command of the English language has led many to believe that he comes from an English-speaking country.

Satoshi published the Bitcoin whitepaper and the Bitcoin software. However, the mysterious creator disappeared in 2010.

## Satoshi did not invent the blockchain

Bitcoin combines a number of technologies that have been around for some time. However, as we have seen the concept blockchain did not originate with Bitcoin. The use of immutable data structures like this can be traced back to the early 1990s when Stuart Haber and W. Scott Stornetta proposed a system for time stamping documents. Just like today's blockchains, it relied on cryptographic techniques to protect data and prevent it from being tampered with.

It is interesting to note that Satoshi's whitepaper does not use the term "blockchain" even once.

## Digital money before Bitcoin

Bitcoin was not the first attempt in the field of digital money, but it is certainly the most successful. Some previous projects paved the way for Satoshi's invention. These are the most famous "Bitcoin before Bitcoin" projects.

## DigiCash

DigiCash was a company founded by cryptographer and computer scientist David Chaum in the late 1980s. It was introduced as a privacy-oriented solution for online transactions, based on a document written by Chaum.
The DigiCash model was a centralized system, but it remains an interesting experiment nonetheless. The company went bankrupt due to the fact that at that moment the world was not ready for digital money.

## B-money

B-money was initially featured in a proposal from computer engineer Wei Dai, published in the 1990s. It was mentioned in the Bitcoin whitepaper, and it's not hard to see why.

B-money proposed a Proof of Work system (used in Bitcoin mining) and the use of a distributed database where users sign transactions. A second version of b-money also described an idea similar to staking, a process used in other cryptocurrencies today.

Ultimately, b-money never caught on, as it didn't make it past the planning stage. That said, Bitcoin clearly takes inspiration from the concepts presented by Wei Dai.

## Bit Gold

The similarity between Bit Gold and Bitcoin is such that some believe that its creator, computer expert Nick Szabo, is Satoshi Nakamoto. Basically, Bit Gold consisted of a register that stored strings of data from a Proof of Work operation.

Like B-money, Bit Gold had never been developed further. The similarities between Bit Gold and Bitcoin have nonetheless cemented its status as the "precursor to Bitcoin".

Bitcoin's history is quite amazing if you ask us and it is full of interesting facts and situations. The fact that we still don't know who Satoshi Nakamoto really makes everything even more fascinating.

# Chapter 2 - Bitcoin's tokenomics

Bitcoin has a limited supply, but not all units are already in circulation. The only way to create new coins is through a process called mining - the special mechanism for adding data to the blockchain.

## The maximum number of Bitcoin

The protocol sets the maximum supply for Bitcoin at twenty-one million coins. In 2020, just under 90% of these were generated, but it will take more than a hundred years to produce the rest. This is due to periodic events known as "halving", which gradually reduce the mining reward.

## Bitcoin mining

Through mining, participants add blocks to the blockchain. To do this, they must devote computing power to solve a cryptographic puzzle. As an incentive, there is a reward available to anyone who proposes a valid block.

Generating a block is expensive, while checking if that block is valid is very cheap and simple. If someone tries to cheat with an invalid block, the network immediately rejects it, and the miner will not be able to recover the mining expenses.

The reward is made up of two components: the fees associated with the transactions and the block subsidy. The block subsidy is the only source of "new" bitcoins there is in the system. With each block mined, the software adds a fixed amount of coins to the total supply.

## How long does it take to mine a block?

The protocol adjusts the mining difficulty to keep mining speed at around ten minutes per new block. Blocks aren't always found exactly ten minutes after the previous one and the time it takes fluctuates around this goal.

# Chapter 3 - How to Buy Bitcoin

The exchange we recommend you to use if you want to invest or trade cryptocurrency is called Binance. Binance allows you to easily buy Bitcoins from your browser. To do it, just follow these steps.

- Go to the Buy and Sell Cryptocurrency portal.
- Select the cryptocurrency you want to buy, and the currency you want to pay with.
- Log in to Binance, or register if you don't have an account yet.
- Select your payment method.
- If prompted, enter your card details and complete identity verification.
- Done! Your bitcoins will be credited to your Binance account.

Buying Bitcoin is extremely easy nowadays and there are a lot of good services that you can use to do it. However, Binance is our favourite exchange, because it offers a wide range of coins to choose from.

## Paying with Bitcoin

There are many things you can buy using Bitcoin. At the present stage, it can be difficult (but not impossible) to find merchants who accept Bitcoin in brick-and-mortar stores. However, you can still find websites that accept it or allow you to use it to buy gift cards for other services.

Just to name a few, you can use Bitcoin to buy:

- Airline tickets
- Hotel rooms
- Real estate properties
- Food and beverages
- Clothing
- Gift cards
- Online subscriptions

You can spend your bitcoins in an ever-growing number of places! Below we list some of them.

## TravelbyBit

Save on heavy credit card fees when traveling the world! You can book flights and hotels with bitcoin and other cryptocurrencies through TravelbyBit. Register and book using crypto with a 10% discount on your purchase.

## Spendabit

Spendabit is a search engine for products that you can buy with Bitcoin. Just search for what you want to buy to get a list of merchants you can buy it from using bitcoin.

## Coinmap

Search for all cryptocurrency merchants and ATMs in your area. If you are looking forward to spending your bitcoins and are looking for a place to do it, this could be an ideal choice for you.

## Bitrefill

Here you can buy gift cards for hundreds of services and top up your mobile with Bitcoin and other cryptocurrencies. It's pretty simple to use, and you can even use the Lightning Network to pay.

## Losing your Bitcoin

Since there are no banks involved, the responsibility for protecting the coins is yours. Some prefer to keep them on exchanges, while others take them into custody with a variety of wallets. If you use a wallet, it is of fundamental importance to write and keep the seed phrase in order to be able to restore them in case of problems. There are around 3-4 million BTC lost forever, because the owner lost the seed. You can only imagine how much they are worth today. Don't be that guy!

## Can I reverse Bitcoin transactions?

Once the data is added to the blockchain, it is not easy to remove it (in practice, it is virtually impossible). This means that when you make a transaction, it cannot be undone. For this reason, you should always check two or three times that the address you are sending funds to is the right one.

## Can I earn money with Bitcoin?

You can make money with Bitcoin, but you can also lose money. Typically, long-term investors buy and hold Bitcoin in the belief that its price will rise in the future. This is our main strategy and something we really suggest you do on a regular basis if you are interested in the world of cryptocurrency. Other people choose to actively switch between Bitcoin and other cryptocurrencies to make short and medium-term profits. Both strategies are risky, but they are often more rewarding than low-risk approaches.

Some investors adopt hybrid strategies. They store bitcoin as a long-term investment and at the same time trade with a portion of their portfolio. There is no right or wrong when it comes to allocating assets in your portfolio - each investor has a different risk tolerance and different goals.

Lending is an increasingly popular form of passive income in the cryptocurrency world. By lending your coins to someone else, you can generate interest which they will pay later. Platforms like Binance Lending allow you to do this with Bitcoin and other cryptocurrencies.

## Storing your Bitcoin

There are many options for storing coins, each with their own strengths and weaknesses.

## Storing your bitcoins on Binance

A custodial solution refers to storage where the user does not actually own the coins, but trusts a third party to do it for them. To make transactions, they must log into the third party's platform. Exchanges like Binance often use this model as it is much more efficient for operations.

Storing your coins on Binance allows you to easily access them for trading or lending, but there is a risk associated with trusting a third party.

## Storing your coins in a wallet

Non-custodial solutions are the opposite of custodial solutions. In fact, they put the user in control of the funds. A wallet does not directly contain your coins - instead, it contains the cryptographic keys that can unlock them on the blockchain. There are two main options when it comes to wallet.

## Hot wallets

A hot wallet is software that somehow connects to the internet. Generally speaking, it will take the form of a mobile or desktop application that allows you to send and receive coins easily. A simple example of a mobile wallet with many supported coins is MetaMask. Being online, hot wallets are generally more convenient for payments, but they are also more vulnerable to attack.

## Cold wallets

Cryptocurrency wallets that are not exposed to the internet are known as cold wallets. They are less prone to attacks as there cannot be an online attack vector, but as a result they tend to offer a more uncomfortable user experience. Examples in this category include hardware wallets and paper wallets.

# Chapter 4 - The Bitcoin halving

The Bitcoin halving is simply an event that reduces the block reward. Once a halving has occurred, the reward given to miners for validating new blocks is split in two. However, there is no effect on transaction fees.

## How does the Bitcoin halving work?

When Bitcoin was launched, miners were rewarded with 50 BTC for every valid block they found.

The first halving occurred on November 28th, 2012. At that point, the protocol reduced the reward from 50 BTC to 25 BTC. The second halving took place on July 9th, 2016 (from 25 BTC to 12.5 BTC). The third one took place in May 2020 and brought the mining reward to 6.25 BTC.

Perhaps you have noticed a certain pattern. With a difference of a few months, a new halving appears to happen every four years. This is an intentional feature, but the protocol does not set specific dates on which a halving occurs. Instead, it refers to the block number. Every 210,000 blocks, a halving happens. So, we can expect it to take around 2,100,000 minutes for the reward halving, since it takes around 10 minutes to mine a block.

## The purpose of the halving

The halving is one of Bitcoin's core strengths, but Satoshi Nakamoto has never fully explained the reasoning that led him to limit supply to twenty-one million units. Some speculate that it is simply the result of starting with a reward of 50 BTC per block, halved every 210,000 blocks.

Having a limited supply means that the currency is not susceptible to devaluation in the long run. It is in stark contrast to fiat money, which loses purchasing power over time as new units enter circulation.

It makes sense that there are limits on how quickly participants can mine coins. After all, 50% was generated before block 210,000 (that is, before 2012). Had the reward remained the same, all units would have been in circulation as early as 2016.

With the halving mechanism, mining continues to have an incentive for the next 100+ years. This gives the system more than enough time to attract users to develop a commission market.

## The impact of the Bitcoin halving

The biggest impact of halvings falls on miners, as the reward makes up a significant portion of their income. When halved, they only receive half of the previous units. The reward also comprised transaction fees, but to date these make up only a fraction of the block reward.

Therefore, halvings could make it disadvantageous for some participants to continue mining. What this means for the sector as a whole is still unknown. A reduction in rewards could lead to greater centralization in mining pools, or it could simply promote more efficient mining practices.

If Bitcoin continues to rely on a Proof of Work algorithm, the fees should increase to keep mining profitable. This scenario is perfectly possible, as blocks can contain a limited number of transactions. If there are many pending transactions, the ones with the highest fees will be included first.

Historically, a halving is followed by a sharp rise in the price of Bitcoin. Obviously, there isn't much data available as we've only seen three halvings so far. Many attribute the price movement to an appreciation of the scarcity of Bitcoin by the market, a realization triggered by the halving. Proponents of this theory believed the value would have risen again following the May 2020 event. They were right.

Other people disagree with this logic, arguing that the market has already considered the halving. This is also called the Efficient Market Hypothesis. The event comes as no surprise - attendees have known for a decade now that the reward would be reduced every 4 years. Another point is that the crypto industry was extremely underdeveloped during the first two halvings. Currently, the sector has a higher profile, offers sophisticated trading tools and is more open to a larger pool of investors.

# Chapter 5 - Common Questions Beginners Have About Bitcoin

There are a number of questions beginners have when they first approach the world of cryptocurrency. In this chapter we will try to answer some of the most common ones.

## Is Bitcoin anonymous?

Not exactly. Bitcoin may appear anonymous at first glance, but this is incorrect. The Bitcoin blockchain is public and anyone can see the transactions. Your identity is not connected to your wallet addresses on the blockchain, but an observer with the right resources could potentially find a connecion. It is more accurate to describe Bitcoin as a pseudonym. Bitcoin addresses are visible to everyone, but the names of their owners are not.

That said, the system is relatively private, and there are methods to make it even more difficult to understand what you are doing with your bitcoins. Freely available technologies can create a plausible deniability to "break the link" between addresses. Additionally, future updates could significantly increase privacy.

## Is Bitcoin a Scam?

No. Just like a fiat currency, Bitcoin can also be used for illegal activities. However, this doesn't make Bitcoin a scam.

Bitcoin is a digital currency that is not controlled by anyone. Its detractors have labeled it a pyramid scheme, even if it falls outside the definition. As a digital currency, it works at both $20 per coin and $20,000 per coin. It has more than a decade behind it and its technology has proven to be very safe and reliable.

Unfortunately, Bitcoin is used in many scams that you should be aware of. These can include phishing and other social engineering scams, such as fake giveaways and airdrops. As a general rule: if something sounds too good to be true, it's probably a scam. Never give your private keys or seed phrase to anyone, and be wary of schemes that promise to multiply your money with minimal risk. If you send your coins to a scammer or a fake giveaway address, they will be lost forever.

## Is Bitcoin in a bubble?

Over the course of Bitcoin's many parabolic price rises, it was common to see people calling it a speculative bubble. Many economists have compared Bitcoin to periods like Tulipomania or the dot-com boom.

Due to the unique nature of Bitcoin as a decentralized digital product, its price is entirely dictated by speculation in the free market. Therefore, while there are many factors driving Bitcoin's price, they affect the supply and demand of the market. And because Bitcoin is limited and follows a rigid issuance schedule, it is believed that in the long run, demand will outstrip supply.

Cryptocurrency markets are also relatively small compared to traditional markets. This means that Bitcoin and other crypto assets tend to be more volatile, and it is quite common to see short-term disparities between supply and demand in the market.

In other words, Bitcoin can sometimes be a volatile asset. However, volatility is part of any financial market, especially those with relatively lower volume and liquidity.

## Does Bitcoin use encryption?

No. This is a common misconception. The Bitcoin blockchain does not use encryption. Every participant in the network must be able to read the transactions to ensure they are valid. Instead, it uses digital signatures and hash functions. While some digital signature algorithms use encryption, this is not the case with Bitcoin.

However, it is worth noting that many applications and crypto wallets use encryption to protect users' wallets with passwords. Nonetheless, these coding methods have nothing to do with the blockchain. They are just being incorporated into other technologies that make use of it.

## What is scalability?

Scalability is a measure of a system's ability to scale up to meet growing demand. If you manage a website overloaded with requests, you could scale it by adding more servers. If you want to run more intensive applications on your computer, you might want to improve its components.

In the context of cryptocurrencies, we use the term to describe how easily a blockchain can be improved to be able to process a higher number of transactions over a period of time.

## Why does Bitcoin need to scale?

To work in daily payments, Bitcoin needs to be fast. At present, it has a relatively low throughput, which means that a limited number of transactions can be processed per block.

As we explained in the previous chapter, miners receive transaction fees as part of the reward for each block. Users associate these fees with their transactions to incentivize miners to add them to the blockchain.

Miners seek to make a return on their investment in hardware and electricity, so they prioritize transactions with the highest fees. If there are many transactions in the network "waiting for space" (they are said to be in the mempool), the fees can increase significantly as users bid more to be able to include their own. In the worst times, the average commission was over $50 per transaction. What it is important to note here is that transaction fees do not depend on the value of the transaction. If you are transferring millions of dollars, you might be comfortable with spending $50 to complete the transaction. On the other hand, if you are purchasing a 5$ coffee, that would be 1000% of the transaction value.

## How many transactions can Bitcoin process?

Based on the average number of transactions per block, Bitcoin can currently handle around five transactions per second. It is a much lower figure than with centralized payment solutions, but this is one of the costs of a decentralized currency.

Since it is not managed by a datacenter that can be updated at will by a single entity, Bitcoin must limit the size of its blocks. A new block size that allows 10,000 transactions per second could be integrated, but it would damage the decentralization of the network. Remember that full nodes have to download new information about every ten minutes. If it becomes too expensive to do so, they are likely to go offline.

To use the protocol in payments, Bitcoin enthusiasts believe that effective scaling must be achieved in different ways.

## What is the Lightning Network?

The Lightning Network is a proposed scalability solution for Bitcoin. We call it a layer two solution because it moves transactions out of the blockchain. Instead of recording all transactions on the base layer, they are handled by another protocol developed on top of it.

The Lightning Network allows users to send funds almost instantly and for free. There are no throughput limits (as long as users have the ability to send and receive). To use the Bitcoin Lightning Network, two participants block some of their coins in a special address. The address has a unique property - it only releases bitcoins if both parties agree.

From here, the two sides maintain a private ledger that can reallocate budgets without announcing it to the main chain. They only post a transaction on the blockchain when they are done. At this point the protocol updates their budgets appropriately. Note that the two parties must not trust each other. If either of them tries to cheat, the protocol will detect it and punish it.

A payment channel like this only requires two on-chain transactions from the user - one to fund the address and one to distribute the coins at the end of the off-chain transaction series. This means that thousands of transactions can be made in the meantime. With further development and optimization, the technology could become a key component of large blockchain systems.

## What is a Bitcoin node?

"Bitcoin Node" is a term used to describe a program that interacts with the Bitcoin network in some way. It can be anything from a mobile phone with a Bitcoin wallet to a dedicated computer that keeps a full copy of the blockchain.

There are several types of nodes, each of which performs specific functions. All act as a point of communication to the network. Within the system, they transmit information relating to transactions and blocks.

## How does a Bitcoin full node work?

A full node validates transactions and locks if certain requirements are met. Most full nodes run the Bitcoin Core software, the reference implementation of the Bitcoin protocol.

Bitcoin Core is the program released by Satoshi Nakamoto in 2009 - it was simply called Bitcoin at the time, but was later renamed to avoid confusion with forked chains. Other implementations can also be used, as long as they are compatible with Bitcoin Core.

Full nodes are important for Bitcoin decentralization. They download and validate blocks and transactions, and propagate them to the rest of the network. Since they independently verify the authenticity of the information they receive, the user does not have to rely on a third party for anything.

If a full node stores a complete copy of the blockchain, it is referred to as a full archivil node. Some users delete older blocks, to save space. In fact, the Bitcoin blockchain contains more than 200GB of transaction data.

## What is a Bitcoin light node?

Light nodes have less functionality than full nodes, but they also require fewer resources to operate. They allow users to interface with the network without performing all the operations of a full node.

While a full node downloads all blocks to validate them, light nodes download only a portion of each block (called the block header). Even though the block header is very small, it contains information that allows users to check that their transactions are in a specific block.

Light nodes are ideal for devices with bandwidth or space constraints. It is common to find this type of node on desktop and mobile wallets. Since they cannot validate transactions, light nodes depend on full nodes.

## What is a mining node?

Mining nodes are full nodes that perform an additional task - they produce blocks. As we have already mentioned, they require specialized equipment and software to add data to the blockchain.

Mining nodes take pending transactions and hash them along with other information to generate a number. If the number is less than a target set by the protocol, the block is valid and can be passed on to other full nodes.

In order to be able to mine without relying on others, miners must run a full node. Otherwise, they cannot know which transactions to include in the block.

If a participant wants to mine without using a full node, they can connect to a server that provides them with the information they need. If you are mining in a pool (i.e., working together with other miners), only one person needs to run a full node.

# Chapter 6 - Bitcoin Mining

A full node can be beneficial for developers, merchants, and end users. Running a Bitcoin Core client on your own hardware offers privacy and security benefits, as well as strengthening the Bitcoin network as a whole. With a full node, you no longer have to rely on others to interact with the ecosystem.

A handful of Bitcoin companies offer plug-and-play nodes. These are pre-built hardware that is shipped to the users, who just need to turn it on to start downloading the blockchain. This may be more convenient for less technical users, but it is often much more expensive than setting one up on your own.

In most cases, an old PC or laptop will suffice. We do not recommend running a node on your everyday computer as it may slow it down considerably. The blockchain is growing all the time, so you will need to make sure you have enough memory to download it in its entirety.

A 1TB hard drive will be enough for the next few years, provided there isn't a big change in the block size. Other requirements to run a full node include 2GB of RAM (most computers have more than this by default) and lots of bandwidth.

## How to mine Bitcoin

In the early days of Bitcoin, it was possible to create new blocks using conventional laptops. The system was unknown at that point, so there was minimal competition in mining. Since the activity was so limited, the protocol naturally set a low mining difficulty.

As the network's hash rate increased, participants had to upgrade their equipment to remain competitive. By going through various types of hardware, the mining industry has eventually entered the era of Application-Specific Integrated Circuits (ASICs).

As the name suggests, these devices are created with a specific purpose: mining Bitcoin. They are extremely efficient, but they can only perform one task. Hence, an ASIC mining is a specialized computer that is used for mining and nothing else. A Bitcoin ASIC can mine Bitcoin, but it cannot mine coins that don't use the same algorithm.

Today, Bitcoin mining requires a significant investment. At the time of writing, a good mining device performs over ten trillion operations per second. While very efficient, ASIC miners consume huge amounts of electricity. Unless you have several low-cost mining rigs and electricity, it is unlikely that you will be able to profit from Bitcoin mining.

However, with the necessary materials, setting up your mining operation is relatively simple. Many ASICs come with their own software. The most popular option is to point your miners to a mining pool, where you work together with others to find blocks. If you are successful, you will receive part of the block reward proportional to the hash rate you provided.

You can also choose to mine alone, working by yourself. The probability of generating a block will be lower, but you will receive the full reward if you create a valid block.

## How long does it take to mine a bitcoin?

It is difficult to give a one-size-fits-all answer, as there are several variables to consider. How quickly you can mine a coin depends on the amount of electricity and hash rate at your disposal. You will also need to calculate the costs of actually operating a mining device.

To get an idea of the revenue generated from Bitcoin mining, it is recommended to use a mining calculator to estimate costs. You can find a mining calculator at nicehash.com.

## Contributing to the Bitcoin code

The Bitcoin Core software is open-source, which means anyone can contribute to it. You can propose or review new features to add to the 70,000+ lines of code. You can also report bugs, or translate and improve the documentation.

Software changes go through a rigorous review process. After all, software that manages hundreds of billions of dollars in value must be free of any vulnerabilities and need the consensus of at least 51% of the miners.

# Chapter 7 - What is Ethereum?

As we have done for Bitcoin, we will dedicate the next few chapters to the explanation of the second largest cryptocurrency. We are talking about the mother of smart contracts: Ethereum. This section is extremely important, as it will help you understand the more complicated DeFi projects we will discuss later on. Pay attention to the next few pages.

Ethereum is a decentralized IT platform. You can see it as a laptop or a PC, but it doesn't run on a single device. Instead, it works simultaneously on thousands of devices around the world, which means it doesn't have an owner.

Ethereum, like Bitcoin and other cryptocurrencies, allows you to transfer digital money. However, it is capable of much more. You can implement your own code, and interact with applications created by other users. Thanks to its flexibility, all sorts of sophisticated programs can be launched on Ethereum.

Simply put, the central idea behind Ethereum is that developers can create and implement code that runs across a distributed network, rather than existing on a centralized server. This means that, in theory, these applications cannot be blocked or censored.

## The difference between Ethereum and ETH

It might be counterintuitive, but the units used in Ethereum are not called Ethereum or Ethereums. Ethereum is the protocol itself, but the currency that makes it work is simply known as ether (or ETH).

## What makes Ethereum valuable?

We mentioned the idea that Ethereum can execute code through a distributed system. Therefore, programs cannot be altered by external parties. They are added to the Ethereum database (i.e., the blockchain), and can be programmed so that the code cannot be changed. Also, the database is visible to everyone, so users can verify the code before interacting with it.

This means that anyone can launch applications that cannot be disabled. Even more interesting, since its native unit holds value, these applications can set conditions on how the value is passed. We call the programs that make up these applications "smart contracts". In most cases, they can be configured to operate without human intervention.

Understandably, the idea of "programmable money" has attracted users, developers and companies all over the world.

## Ethereum vs. Bitcoin

Bitcoin relies on blockchain technology and financial incentives to create a global digital currency system. It has introduced some key innovations that allow coordination of users around the world without the need for a central organizer. As each participant runs a program on their computer, Bitcoin has made it possible for users to agree on the status of a financial database in a trustless and decentralized context.

Bitcoin is often regarded as a first generation blockchain. It was not created as an overly complex system, which turns out to be a strong point when it comes to security. It is intentionally kept inflexible to prioritize safety at its base level. Because of this, the smart contract language in Bitcoin is extremely limited, and cannot host applications outside of transactions very well.

The second generation of blockchain, on the other hand, is capable of doing more. In addition to financial transactions, these platforms allow for a greater degree of programmability. Ethereum gives developers much more freedom to experiment with their code and create what we call Decentralized Applications (DApps).

Ethereum was the first in the wave of second generation blockchains and remains the most prominent to this day. It bears similarities to Bitcoin and can perform many of the same functions. However, the two are actually very different, and each has its own advantages over the other.

## How Ethereum works

We can define Ethereum as a "state machine". This simply means that, at any given time, you have a snapshot of all account balances and smart contracts as they currently appear. Some actions will cause the status to update, so all nodes will update their snapshot to reflect the change.

Smart contracts executed on Ethereum are triggered by transactions (whether by users or by other contracts). When a user submits a transaction to a contract, each node on the network executes the contract code and logs the output. To do this, it uses the Ethereum Virtual Machine (EVM), which converts smart contracts into computer-readable instructions.
To update the status, Ethereum uses a special mechanism called mining. Mining follows a Proof of Work algorithm, similar to that of Bitcoin. We will explore this topic shortly.

## What is a smart contract?

A smart contract is simply a piece of code. The code is neither "smart" nor a contract in the traditional sense. We call it smart as it performs itself under certain conditions, and it can be considered a contract as it enforces agreements between the parties.

The idea, proposed in the late 1990s, is attributed to the computer scientist Nick Szabo. He used the example of a vending machine to explain the concept, claiming it could be seen as a precursor to the modern smart contract. In the case of the vending machine, the executed contract is simple. Users insert coins and, in return, the machine dispenses a product of their choice.

A smart contract applies this type of logic in a digital context. You could specify something simple in the code like: return "Hello, World!" when two ethers are sent to this contract.

On Ethereum, the developer could program the contract so that it can later be read by the EVM. They can then publish it by sending it to a special address that records the contract. At that point, anyone can use it, and the contract can't be deleted, unless the developer specified a deleting condition when writing the code.

Now, the contract has an address. To interact with it, users simply need to send 2 ETH to that address. This will activate the contract code - all computers on the network will execute it, see that payment has been made to the contract and log the output ("Hello, World!").

What we have described above is perhaps one of the most basic examples of what is possible with Ethereum. Of course, more sophisticated applications linking different contracts can be built.

## The creator of Ethereum

As you know, in 2008 an unknown developer (or group of developers) published the Bitcoin whitepaper under the pseudonym of Satoshi Nakamoto. This has permanently changed the digital money landscape. A few years later, a young developer named Vitalik Buterin devised a way to delve into this idea and apply it to any type of application. The concept was concretized in Ethereum.

Ethereum was proposed by Buterin in a blog post dating back to 2013 entitled "Ethereum: The Ultimate Smart Contract and Decentralized Application Platform". In his post, he described the idea for a Turing-complete blockchain - a decentralized computer that, with enough time and resources, could run any application.

Over time, the types of applications that could be implemented on the blockchain would only be limited by the imagination of developers. Ethereum aims to find out if blockchain technology has valid uses outside of Bitcoin's intentional design boundaries.

## ETH distribution

Ethereum was launched in 2015 with an initial supply of 72 million ether. Over 50 million of these tokens were distributed in a public token sale called the Initial Coin Offering (ICO), in which those interested in participating could buy ether tokens in exchange for bitcoin or fiat currencies.

## The DAO and Ethereum Classic

With Ethereum, completely new ways of open collaboration over the internet have become possible. Take, for example, DAOs (decentralized autonomous organizations), entities governed by computer code, similar to a computer program.

One of the first and most ambitious attempts of this organization was "The DAO". It would have consisted of complex smart contracts running on top of Ethereum, functioning as a standalone venture fund. DAO tokens were distributed during an ICO, giving token holders an ownership stake, along with voting rights.

However, shortly after its launch, hackers exploited a vulnerability and managed to drain nearly a third of DAO's funds. At that time, 14% of the entire ether supply was blocked in the DAO. Obviously, this was a devastating event for the young Ethereum network.

Following some discussion, the chain was hard forked, splitting into two different blockchains. In one of them, the hackers' transactions were actually "reversed" to restore the funds - this chain is what we know today as the Ethereum blockchain. The original chain, in which transactions were not reversed, and immutability was maintained, is now known as Ethereum Classic.

The event became a stark reminder of the risks of this technology, and how putting large amounts of value into a standalone code can have adverse consequences. It is also an interesting example of the significant challenges that arise from collective decisions. However, disregarding its security vulnerabilities, The DAO perfectly illustrated the potential of smart contracts in enabling large-scale trustless collaboration across the Internet.

# Chapter 8 - ETH Tokenomics

If you are familiar with Bitcoin, you will know that the mining process is integral to protecting and updating the blockchain. In Ethereum, the same principle applies: to reward users for mining (an expensive process), the protocol distributes ether.

## Total supply

As of April 2021, the total supply of ether is approximately 115 million.

Unlike Bitcoin, the token issuance schedule was intentionally left indefinite at launch. Bitcoin has set out to preserve value by limiting its supply, and slowly reducing the amount of new coins coming into circulation. Ethereum, on the other hand, aims to provide a foundation for decentralized applications (DApps). As it is unclear which token issuance program is best suited for this purpose, the question remains open.

## Ethereum mining

Mining is critical to network security. It ensures that the blockchain is updated following the rules and allows the network to function without a central organizer. In mining, a subset of nodes (called miners) devote computational power to solving a cryptographic puzzle.

What they are actually doing is hashing a set of pending transactions, along with other data. For the block to be considered valid, the hash must be less than a protocol-defined value. If the miners are unsuccessful, they can modify some of the data and try again.

To compete with others, miners must therefore be able to generate hashes as fast as possible - we measure their power in hash rates. The higher the hash rate on the network, the more difficult the puzzle to solve will be. Only miners need to find the solution. Once they have found it, it is easy for other participants to check that it is valid.

As you can imagine, continuous hashing at high speeds is expensive. To incentivize miners to protect the network, a reward is distributed, consisting of all transaction fees in the block. Plus, they receive freshly generated ether - 2 ETH at the time of writing.

## Ethereum gas?

Remember the "Hello, World!" Contract that we mentioned earlier? It is a very simple program to run, it does not require too many computational resources. However, you're not just running it on your PC - you're also asking everyone in the Ethereum ecosystem to run it.

This leads us to the following question. What happens when tens of thousands of people are executing sophisticated contracts? If someone sets up their contract to keep repeating the same code, each node will have to execute it indefinitely. This would require too many resources and the system would likely collapse.

Fortunately, Ethereum introduces the concept of gas to mitigate this risk. Just as your car doesn't run without gas, contracts can't be executed without gas. Contracts define a quantity of gas that users must pay for in order to successfully execute them. If there is not enough gas, the contract will stop running.

In essence, it is a commission mechanism. The same concept extends to transactions. Miners are primarily motivated by profit, so they may ignore transactions with a lower fee.

Remember that ether and gas are not the same. The average gas price fluctuates and is mainly decided by the miners. When you make a transaction, you pay for gas in ETH. In this context, it is similar to Bitcoin's fees - if the network is clogged and many users are trying to transact, the average gas price is likely to rise. Conversely, if the activity is scarce, the gas price will decrease.

Although the price of gas varies, each operation requires a fixed amount of gas. This means that complex contracts will consume much more than just a simple transaction. Hence, gas is a measure of computational power. It ensures that the system can present an appropriate fee to users based on their use of Ethereum assets.

Typically, gas costs a fraction of ether. Consequently, we use a smaller unit (gwei) to indicate this. One gwei corresponds to one billionth of an ether.

Simply put, you could be running a program that repeats itself for a long time. However, doing so will quickly become very expensive.

## Gas limits

Suppose Alice is making a transaction towards a contract, and she has calculated how much she wants to spend on gas. She may choose a higher price to incentivize miners to include her transaction as quickly as possible.

But she will also set a gas limit to protect herself. Something could go wrong with the contract, leading to it consuming more gas than she anticipated. The gas limit is set to ensure that once a certain quantity of gas is used, the operation is stopped. The contract will be blocked, but Alice will not end up paying more than she initially decided.

At first glance it might seem like a difficult concept to understand. Don't worry - you can manually set the price you want to pay for gas (and the gas limit), but most wallets will take care of that for you. In short, the gas price defines how quickly miners will include your transaction, and the gas limit defines the maximum amount you will pay to include said transaction.

## How long does it take to mine an Ethereum block?

The average time it takes to add a new block to the chain is 12-19 seconds. This interval will most likely change once the network makes the transition to Proof of Stake, which aims, among other things, to make faster block times possible. More on that later.

## Ethereum tokens

A good part of Ethereum's appeal is the ability for users to create their own on-chain assets, which can be stored and transferred as ether. The rules that govern them are defined in smart contracts, allowing developers to set specific parameters for their tokens. These can include the number to be issued, the methods of issue, divisibility, fungibility and many others. The most widely used technical standard that allows for the creation of Ethereum tokens is called ERC-20. This is why tokens are commonly known as ERC-20 tokens.

Token functionality gives innovators a vast playground to experiment with cutting-edge applications in finance and technology. From issuing tokens that act as an in-app currency, to producing unique tokens backed by physical assets, there is great flexibility in design. It is perfectly possible that some of the best use cases for straightforward and easy token creation have not yet been discovered.

# Chapter 9 - How to Buy ETH

In order to buy ETH, we will use the same exchange we did for Bitcoin. In fact, Binance allows you to easily buy ETH from your browser. To do it, you just need to follow these steps.

- Go to the Buy and Sell Cryptocurrency portal.

- Select the cryptocurrency you want to buy (ETH), and the currency you want to pay with.

- Log in to Binance, or register if you don't have an account.

- Select your payment method.

- If prompted, enter your card details and complete the identity verification process.

- Done! Your ETH will be credited to your Binance account.

## Using ETH

Unlike Bitcoin, Ethereum is not designed to be used solely as a cryptocurrency network. It is a platform for building decentralized applications, and as a tradable token, ether is the fuel of this ecosystem. Hence, the primary use case for ether is undoubtedly the utility it offers within the Ethereum network.

That said, ether can also be used in a similar way to a traditional coin, so you can buy goods and services with ETH as with any other currency.

## The use case for Ethereum

People can use Ethereum's native currency, ETH, as a digital currency or as collateral. Many also see it as a store of value, similar to Bitcoin. However, unlike Bitcoin, the Ethereum blockchain is more programmable, so you can do a lot more with ETH. It can be used as the lifeblood for decentralized financial applications, decentralized markets, exchanges, video games and more.

## Losing your ETH

Since there are no banks involved, you are in charge of your own ETH. You can store the coins on an exchange, or in a wallet. It is important to remember that if you use a wallet, you absolutely must take care of your seed phrase. Keep it safe, as you will need it to restore your funds in case you lose access to the wallet.

## Reversing Ethereum transactions

Once the data is added to the Ethereum blockchain, it is virtually impossible to modify or remove it. This means that when you make a transaction, it is considered to be set in stone. For this reason, you should always check several times that the address you are sending funds to is the right one. If you are sending a large amount, it may be useful to send a smaller amount first to make sure the address is correct.

That said, due to a hack against a smart contract, Ethereum performed a hard fork in 2016, in which malicious transactions were effectively "reversed". However, it was an extreme measure taken for an exceptional event and it won't happen again.

## Are Ethereum transactions private?

No. All transactions that are added to the Ethereum blockchain are publicly visible. Even if your real name isn't printed on your Ethereum address, an observer could link it to your identity through other methods.

## Making money with Ethereum

Being a volatile asset, you can make money with ETH just as you can lose money with it. Some prefer to keep ether for the long term, betting on the future of the network as a global programmable level of regulation. Others decide to trade it for other altcoins. However, both strategies involve financial risks.

As the backbone of the Decentralized Finance (DeFi) movement, ETH can also be used to lend, as collateral for borrowing, issuing synthetic assets and - in the future - for staking.

Some investors may hold a long-term position in Bitcoin, without including any other digital assets in their portfolio. Conversely, others may choose to keep ETH and other altcoins in their portfolio, or allocate a certain percentage to shorter-term trading (e.g., day trading or swing trading) as well. There is no one-size-fits-all approach to making money in the cryptocurrency market, and each investor should decide for themselves which strategy is best suited to their risk profile and circumstances.

## Why does Ethereum need to scale?

Ethereum supporters believe the next iteration of the internet will be developed on the platform. The so-called Web 3.0 would introduce a decentralized topology characterized by the absence of intermediaries, a particular attention to privacy and a transition towards the effective ownership of one's data. This foundation would be built using distributed computational resources in the form of smart contracts and distributed storage / communication protocols.

However, to achieve this, Ethereum must significantly increase the number of transactions it can process without harming the decentralization of the network. At the moment, Ethereum does not stem the volume of transactions by limiting block sizes like Bitcoin does. Instead, it imposes a gas limit per block. Only a certain amount of gas can be included in a block.

For example, if you have a gas limit per block of 100,000 gwei and want to include ten transactions with a gas limit of 10,000 gwei each, no problem. The same goes for two 50,000 gwei transactions. Any other transactions presented together with these will have to wait for the next block.

This process is not ideal for a system that everyone is using. If there are more transactions pending than the space available in a block, a backlog will form in no time. The price of gas will rise, and users will have to bid more than others to get their transactions included first. Depending on how crowded the network is, operations may become too expensive for some use cases.

For instance, CryptoKitties' surge in popularity was a prime example of Ethereum's limitations in this respect. In 2017, the Ethereum-based game prompted many users to transact to participate in the breeding of digital cats (represented as non-fungible tokens). The game has become so popular that pending transactions have skyrocketed, resulting in extreme network congestion for some time.

# Chapter 10 - The Blockchain Scalability Trilemma

It seems that a simple increase in the gas limit per block would alleviate all the scalability problems on ETH. The higher the maximum level, the greater the number of transactions that can be processed in a given period, right?

Unfortunately, this solution is not viable without sacrificing other fundamental Ethereum properties. Vitalik Buterin proposed the Blockchain Trilemma to explain the delicate balance that blockchains must maintain.

By choosing to optimize two of three properties between security, decentralization and scalability, the third will lag behind. Blockchains like Ethereum and Bitcoin prioritize security and decentralization. Their consensus algorithms ensure the security of networks, which are made up of thousands of nodes, but this also leads to poor scalability. With such a large number of nodes receiving and validating transactions, the system is much slower than those offered by centralized alternatives.

In another scenario, the gas limit per block could be removed so that the network gains security and scalability, but it will not have the same degree of decentralization.

This is because multiple transactions in a block result in larger blocks. Nodes in the network must download and propagate blocks periodically, and this process is hardware intensive. As the gas limit per block is increased, it becomes more difficult for nodes to validate, store and transmit blocks.

As a result, it is likely that a percentage of the nodes would fail to continue and leave the network. By continuing this way, only a fraction of powerful nodes would be able to participate. This would lead to greater centralization. We could come up with a secure and scalable blockchain, but it wouldn't be decentralized.

Finally, we can imagine a blockchain that focuses on decentralization and scalability. To be fast and decentralized at the same time, sacrifices are required regarding the consensus algorithm used, leading to weaker security.

## How many transactions can Ethereum process?

In recent years, Ethereum has rarely exceeded ten transactions per second (TPS). For a platform aiming to become a "global computer", this number is surprisingly low.

However, the Ethereum roadmap does include scalability solutions. Plasma is an example of a scaling solution. It aims to increase the efficiency of Ethereum, but the technique can also be applied to other blockchain networks.

# Chapter 11 - Ethereum 2.0

Despite its potential, Ethereum currently has significant limitations. We have already talked about the problem of scalability. In short, if Ethereum is to become the backbone of the new financial system, it must be able to process many more transactions per second. Considering the distributed nature of its network, this is an immensely difficult problem to solve, and Ethereum developers have been working on it for years.

First, limits must be imposed to maintain sufficient decentralization. The higher the requirements to operate a node, the fewer participants there will be, and the more centralized the network will become. Hence, increasing the number of transactions that Ethereum can process could threaten the integrity of the system, as it would also increase the load on the nodes.

Another criticism of Ethereum is the sheer amount of resources required. To be able to successfully add a block to the blockchain, mining is required. To create a block in this way, nodes must quickly perform computations that consume huge amounts of electricity.

To address the limitations described above, a major set of updates have been proposed, collectively known as Ethereum

2.0 (or ETH 2.0). Once fully launched, ETH 2.0 is expected to dramatically improve network performance.

## Ethereum sharding

As mentioned above, each node keeps a copy of the entire blockchain. Each time it is extended, each node has to update it, consuming bandwidth and available memory.

Using a method called sharding, this may no longer be necessary. The name refers to the process of dividing the network into subsets of nodes. These are called shards. Each of these shards will process their own transactions and contracts, but will still be able to communicate with the general shard network as required. Since each shard validated independently, it is no longer necessary to retain data from other shards.

Sharding is one of the more complex approaches to scalability, and requires a lot of design and implementation work. However, if implemented successfully, it would also be one of the most effective updates, increasing the network's capabilities by entire orders of magnitude.

## Ethereum Plasma

Ethereum Plasma is what we call an off-chain scaling solution. As we have seen before, off-chain scaling solutions aim to improve processing capabilities by moving transactions outside the blockchain. In this sense, it has some similarities with side chains and payment channels.

With Plasma, secondary chains are anchored to the main Ethereum blockchain, even though they keep communication to a minimum. They operate more or less independently, but users still depend on the main chain to resolve disputes or "complete" their activities on the secondary chains.

Reducing the amount of data nodes need to hold is vital to Ethereum's scalability. Plasma's approach allows developers to delineate the operation of "child" chains in a smart contract on the main chain. After that, they are free to build applications with information or processes that would be too expensive to store / run on the main chain.

## Ethereum rollups

Rollups are similar to Plasma in that they aim to improve Ethereum by moving transactions outside the main blockchain. So how do they work?

A single contract on the main chain holds all funds on the secondary chain and maintains cryptographic proof of the current state of the chain. The operators of this secondary chain, who set a constraint in the mainnet contract, ensure that only valid state transitions are sent to the mainnet contract. The idea is that by keeping this off-chain state, there is no need to store data on the blockchain. The central difference between rollup and Plasma, however, lies in the way transactions are sent to the main chain. By using a special transaction type, it is possible to "bundle" a large number of transactions together within a special block called the Rollup block.

There are two types of rollups: Optimistic and ZK Rollup. Both ensure the correctness of state transitions in different ways.

## ZK Rollups

ZK Rollups submit transactions using a cryptographic verification method called zero-knowledge proof. Specifically, an approach to it called zk-SNARK. We won't go into detail on how it works in this chapter, but how it can be used for rollups. It is a way to show the different participants that they have a particular information without revealing what that information is.

In the case of ZK Rollups, this information is the state transitions sent to the main chain. A big advantage of this method is that the process can take place almost instantaneously, and there is virtually no possibility of sending compromised states to the chain.

## Optimistic Rollups

Optimistic Rollups sacrifice some scalability for greater flexibility. Using a virtual machine called the Optimistic Virtual Machine (OVM), they allow you to run smart contracts on these secondary chains. However, there is no cryptographic evidence that the state transition sent to the main chain is correct. To mitigate this, a slight delay is enforced to allow users to challenge and reject invalid blocks sent to the main chain.

## Proof of Stake (PoS)

Proof of Stake (PoS) is an alternative method to Proof of Work for block validation. In a Proof of Stake system, blocks are not mined, but minted. Instead of miners competing with computational power, a node (or validator) is chosen periodically to validate a candidate block. If done correctly, it will receive all transaction fees contained in the block and, depending on the protocol, possibly even a block reward.

Since mining is no longer used, Proof of Stake is considered less harmful to the environment. Validators consume a fraction of the energy used by miners, and can instead mint blocks on common hardware.

Ethereum's transition from PoW to PoS is scheduled as part of Ethereum 2.0, with an update known as Casper. While an exact date has not yet been announced, the first iteration is likely to launch in 2021.

## Ethereum staking

In Proof of Work protocols, network security is ensured by miners. Miners will not cheat, as they will waste electricity and lose potential rewards. In Proof of Stake, game theory is not applied, but several crypto economic measures are put in place to ensure network security.

In Proof of Stake, what prevents dishonest behavior is the risk of losing funds. Validators must wager a stake (i.e. a quantity of tokens) to participate in the validation. This is a fixed ether sum that is lost if the node tries to cheat, or is slowly emptied if the node is unresponsive or offline. However, if the validator operates additional nodes, they will get more rewards.

The minimum estimated stake for Ethereum is 32 ETH per validator. This number is so huge to make the cost of attempting a 51% attack extremely high.

## How many ETH can I earn by staking on Ethereum?

It is not a simple question. The gain is based on your stake, but also on the total number of ETH staking on the network and on the inflation rate. As a very rough estimate, current calculations predict annual returns of 6%. Remember this is only an estimate and may change in the future.

## How long do I have to block my ETH for staking?

There will be a queue to withdraw your ETH from your validator. In the absence of this queue, the minimum withdrawal period is 18 hours, dynamically adjusted based on how many validators are withdrawing at any given time.

## Are there any risks in ETH staking?

As a validator with the responsibility of maintaining network security, there are some risks to consider. If your validator node goes offline for an extended period, you could lose a significant portion of your deposit. Also, if your deposit drops below 16 ETH at any time, you will be removed from the group of validators.

Furthermore, it is important to consider a more systematic risk factor. Proof of Stake has never been implemented on such a scale before, so we can't be completely sure it won't fail. Software will always have bugs and vulnerabilities, and this can have a devastating effect, especially when the stakes are worth billions of dollars.

# Chapter 12 - Ethereum and the Casper Update

Casper is the implementation that will eventually convert Ethereum into a Proof of Stake blockchain. Even though Ethereum launched in the summer of 2015 as a Proof of Work system, developers were already planning a long-term transition to the staking-based model. At the end of the transition, mining will no longer be part of the Ethereum network.

To date, we have seen two Casper implementations being developed in the Ethereum ecosystem: Casper CBC and Casper FFG. The CBC version was initially proposed by Ethereum Foundation researcher Vlad Zamfir. Although CBC research initially focused on PoS protocols for public blockchains, it has evolved into a broader field of study, including a set of PoS models.

Casper FFG research is led by Ethereum co-founder Vitalik Buterin. The initial proposal consisted of a hybrid PoW / PoS system, but the implementation is still under discussion, and new proposals could replace it with a pure PoS model.

Casper FFG is the version that will be used for the initial launch of Ethereum 2.0. However, this does not mean that Casper CBC will no longer be needed. In fact, it could end up replacing or complementing Casper FFG in the future. Although both versions were developed for Ethereum, Casper is a PoS model that can be adopted and implemented in other blockchain networks.

## How Casper Works

The transition from Ethereum 1.0 to 2.0 is referred to as the "Serenity" upgrade. It consisted t of three different phases. In its initial phase (Phase 0), a new blockchain called the Beacon Chain was launched. Casper FFG rules guided the consensus mechanism of this new PoS-based blockchain.

Unlike PoW mining, where miners operate specialized and expensive devices to create and validate blocks of transactions, the Casper implementation removed the mining process from Ethereum. Alternatively, the verification and validation of new transaction blocks takes place via block validators, which are selected based on their stake.

In other words, the voting power of each validator is determined by the sum of ETH they put into play. For example, someone who deposited 64 ETH has twice the voting weight than someone who deposited the minimum stake for staking. To become a block validator in the first phase of Serenity, users need to have a minimum stake of 32 ether deposited in a special smart contract based on the old Ethereum blockchain.

Random validator committees are selected to propose new blocks and eventually receive rewards for producing blocks. These rewards consist of transaction fees as there is no block subsidy.

It is important to note, that each PoS implementation may have a different approach, with different reward models. The Casper model is still under development, and many details are yet to be defined.

## Advantages of Casper

One of the benefits of Casper is that by making staking possible, it helps Ethereum go green. When it comes to electricity and computational resources, PoW-based systems are very demanding. Conversely, PoS models have a much lower demand. When a pure PoS model will be fully implemented in Ethereum, miners will no longer be needed to secure the blockchain, so the required resources will be much less.

Another potential benefit of Casper relates to safety. Essentially, Casper can be used as a selector, responsible for sorting the block chain. In practice, it has the function of administrator of the Ethereum 2.0 registry. Therefore, if a validator acts dishonestly, they are quickly removed and punished. The penalty for breaking the rules is the validator stake, so network transgressions are very expensive.

Finally, some argue that Casper can provide Ethereum with greater levels of decentralization. For now, the most powerful participants in the network are those who have the resources to manage mining operations. In the future, anyone who can buy the required amount of ether will be able to help secure their blockchain.

## Limits

In terms of theoretical limitations, Casper is not able to finalize blocks if Ethereum's validation system becomes corrupt. In its current structure, Casper is not entirely resistant to 51% attacks. Furthermore, there is still no formal specification for defining a fork rule that might be needed in the event of an attack.

In short, Casper can create the foundation upon which further advances in Ethereum 2.0 will be built, and can smooth the transition to a PoS model. Furthermore, the open source nature of the blockchain space also implies that Casper's benefits can be replicated, modified and processed by other projects in perpetuity.

We are excited to see Ethereum 2.0 coming out in the coming years.

# Chapter 13 - The Basics of DeFi

Decentralized Finance (or simply, DeFi) is a movement that aims to decentralize financial applications. DeFi is built on public and open source blockchains accessible by anyone with an internet connection. This is a crucial element in potentially introducing billions of people to this new global financial system.

In the growing ecosystem of DeFi, users interact with smart contracts and with each other through peer-to-peer networks and Decentralized Applications (DApps). The great advantage of DeFi is that users still retain ownership of their funds at all times.

Simply put, Decentralized Finance (DeFi) aims to create a new financial ecosystem free from the restrictions of the standard one. Due to its high degree of decentralization and its large developer base, most DeFi applications are currently being built on Ethereum.

## Use cases for decentralized finance (DeFi)

You probably know this already, but one of the main advantages of Bitcoin is that you don't need a central authority to coordinate the operation of the network. But what if we built programmable applications on top of it? This is the potential of

DeFi applications. No central coordinator or intermediary, and no single point of failure.

As mentioned, one of the great advantages of DeFi is free access. There are billions of people around the world who do not have access to any type of financial service. Can you imagine how to manage daily life without the certainty of your finances? There are billions of people living like this. Ultimately, this is DeFi's target demographic.

## Decentralized Finance (DeFi) and the mainstream world

This all sounds great, so why hasn't DeFi taken the world by storm yet? Because currently, most DeFi applications are difficult to use. They are inconvenient and highly experimental. Apparently, even working out the frameworks for this ecosystem is extremely difficult, especially in a distributed development context.

Software engineers, game theory experts, mechanical designers and many others still have a long way to go to solve all the challenges related to building the DeFi ecosystem. As such, it remains to be seen whether DeFi applications will succeed in achieving mainstream adoption or not.

## DApps

One of the most popular use cases for Decentralized Finance (DeFi) are stablecoins. Essentially, they are tokens on a blockchain with a value anchored to a real-world asset, such as a fiat currency. For example, BUSD is pegged to the value of the Dollar. What makes these tokens practical to use is their existence on a blockchain, which makes them very easy to store and transfer.

Loans are another popular type of application. There are many peer-to-peer services that allow you to lend your funds to others and collect the accrued interest. In fact, one of the easiest ways to do this is through Binance Lending. All you have to do is transfer your funds to your loan wallet, and you can start earning interest the next day.

However, probably the most exciting part of DeFi are the hard-to-categorize applications. These can include any kind of decentralized peer-to-peer marketplace, where users can trade unique crypto collectibles and other digital items. They can also allow for the creation of synthetic assets, where anyone can create a market for just about anything that has value. Other uses may include forecasting markets, derivatives, and more.

## Decentralized Exchanges (DEX) on Ethereum

A Decentralized Exchange (DEX) is a platform that allows you to carry out transactions directly between users' wallets. When you trade on Binance or Coinbase, you send your funds to the exchange, and trade through its internal systems.

Decentralized Exchanges are different. Thanks to the magic of smart contracts, they allow you to trade directly from your crypto wallet, eliminating the possibility of hacks to the detriment of the exchange and other risks.

A great example of a decentralized exchange is Binance DEX. Some other notable examples built on Ethereum are Uniswap, Kyber Network, and IDEX. Many of these even allow you to trade from your hardware wallet for maximum security.

As of April 2021, DEXs tend to be the most used applications on the Ethereum blockchain. However, the trading volume is still small when compared to centralized exchanges. Despite this, if DEX developers and designers enrich the user experience to make it more friendly, DEXs could compete with centralized exchanges in the future.

Decentralized Finance evolves so fast that it can be difficult to keep up, or evaluate new projects in good time. What makes this task even more complicated is the absence of a standard approach. In fact, there are numerous different methods for measuring and comparing DeFi protocols.

For this reason, we are about to discuss some commonly used indicators that can be valid sources of information in DeFi. Since a large amount of data is accessible to the public on-chain, it is easy for any trader or investor to use these indicators.

## Total blocked value (TVL)

As the name suggests, Total Blocked Value (TVL) is the aggregate amount of funds blocked in a DeFi protocol. You can think of TVL as all liquidity in the pools of a certain money market. For example, in the case of Uniswap, the TVL represents the amount of funds deposited by liquidity providers in the protocol.

The TVL can be useful information that gives an idea of the overall interest in DeFi. It also allows you to compare the "market share" of different DeFi protocols. This can be especially useful for investors looking for undervalued DeFi projects.

It should also be noted that TVL can be measured using different denominations. For example, TVL locked into Ethereum-based projects is usually measured in ETH or USD.

## Price-to-sales ratio (P / S ratio)

In the case of a more traditional company, the Price-to-Sales Ratio (P / S ratio) compares the company's stock price to its revenue. This ratio is then used to determine whether the stocks are undervalued or overvalued.

Since many DeFi protocols already generate revenue, a similar parameter can be used for them as well. How? By dividing the market capitalization of the protocol by its revenues. The basic idea is that the lower the resulting ratio, the more the protocol is underestimated.

Note that this is not a definitive method of calculating a project valuation. However, it can be useful for providing a general idea of how the market is evaluating a project.

## Offer of tokens on exchanges

Another strategy involves monitoring the token supply on cryptocurrency exchanges. When sellers want to sell tokens, they usually do so on centralized exchanges (CEX). That said, there are more and more options available to users on decentralized exchanges (DEXs) that do not require trust in an intermediary. However, centralized platforms tend to offer much higher liquidity. For this reason it is important to pay attention to the offer of tokens on CEX.

We can make a simple guess about the token offering. When there is a large number of tokens on exchanges, the selling pressure may be higher. Since whales are not holding the funds in their wallets, they may be trying to sell them.

In reality, the matter is not that simple. Many traders use their funds as collateral for trading on margin or futures contracts. Hence, the arrival of a large sum on an exchange does not necessarily mean that a sell-off is approaching. However, it might be useful to keep an eye on this factor.

## Exchange token balance changes

We already know that tracking the token supply can be helpful. However, studying token balances alone may not be enough. Another factor to consider is the recent changes in these balances. Often large changes in token balances on exchanges can signal increased volatility.

For example, consider the opposite scenario to what we described for token balances. If users are withdrawing large sums from the CEX, this could indicate that the whales are accumulating the token. In fact, if they were going to sell shortly, why withdraw from their wallets? This is why monitoring token movements can be useful.

## Number of unique addresses

Despite the limitations of this parameter, a steadily growing number of addresses containing a particular token or coin should indicate increased usage. At first glance, it would appear that the increase in addresses is related to more users and greater adoption.

However, it is possible to fool this measure. Someone could easily create thousands of addresses and distribute funds to them, thus giving the impression of more widespread use. As with any parameter in fundamental analysis, you should compare the number of unique addresses with other factors.

## Non-speculative use

Understanding what the token is used for is critical if you want to determine its true value. Ideally, you would measure this by looking at the number of transactions that are not executed for speculation purposes. This task can be difficult, but a good start would be to analyze transfers that don't involve decentralized or centralized exchanges. The goal is to verify that people are using the token.

## Inflation rate

Another key parameter to keep an eye on is the inflation rate. A small offer now is no guarantee of a small offer forever, especially if new tokens are continuously issued. One of the main features of Bitcoin is the ever-declining inflation rate, which theoretically should prevent existing units from devaluing in the future.

This does not mean that every system should aspire to replicate the scarcity of Bitcoin. Inflation itself isn't necessarily a bad thing, but too much of it could reduce your share of the pie. There is no standardized percentage that is considered "good" or "bad", so it is wise to take this factor into consideration when analyzing other parameters.

# Chapter 14 - Ethereum Nodes

Ethereum Node is a term that can be used to describe a program that interacts in some way with the Ethereum network. An Ethereum node can be anything from a simple smartphone wallet application to a computer that holds the entire copy of the Ethereum blockchain.

All nodes function to some extent as a point of communication, but there are different types of nodes on the Ethereum network.

## How they work

Unlike Bitcoin, Ethereum does not have a single program as a reference implementation. While the Bitcoin ecosystem has Bitcoin Core as its primary software for the nodes, Ethereum has a variety of individual (but compatible) programs based on its white paper. Popular options include Geth and Parity.

## Ethereum full nodes

To interface with the Ethereum network in order to independently validate blockchain data, you need to operate a full node using software such as those mentioned above.

The software will download blocks from other nodes and verify that the included transactions are correct. In addition to this, the software will execute all active smart contracts to ensure that it receives the same information as the other peers. If everything works as it should, we can expect each node to have an identical copy of the blockchain on their device.

Full nodes are essential for Ethereum to function. Without several nodes scattered around the world, the network would lose its properties of resistance to censorship and decentralization.

## Ethereum light nodes

Operating a full node allows you to directly contribute to the health and safety of the network. However, a full node often requires a separate device and occasional maintenance. Light nodes might be a better option for users who can't manage a full node (or prefer not to).

As the name suggests, light nodes are lightweight. They use fewer resources and take up minimal space. For this reason, they can be used on common devices such as smartphones or laptops. This convenience comes at a cost. In fact, light nodes are not entirely self-sufficient. They do not fully synchronize the blockchain and rely on full nodes to obtain relevant information.

Light nodes are popular among merchants, services and users. They are used extensively for making and receiving payments in scenarios where full nodes are considered unnecessary and too expensive to manage.

## Ethereum mining nodes

A mining node can be a full or light node. The term "mining node" is not used as in the Bitcoin ecosystem, but it is still important to describe the operation of these participants.

To mine Ethereum, users need additional hardware. A common practice involves building a mining rig. With these, users connect several GPUs (graphics processing units) together for hashing data at high speeds.

Miners have two options: individual mining or within a mining pool. In individual mining, the miner works alone to create blocks. If successful, they do not share the mining rewards with anyone. The alternative option is to join a mining pool, combining their hashing power with that of other users. This will increase the chances of finding a block, but will also split the reward with pool members.

## How to operate an Ethereum node

One of the most important aspects of blockchains is free access. This means anyone can run an Ethereum node and strengthen the network by validating transactions and blocks.

Similar to Bitcoin, there are several companies that offer plug and play Ethereum nodes. This may be the best option if you want to operate a node as easily as possible. You just need to be prepared to pay extra for the convenience.

As already mentioned, Ethereum has several software implementations for nodes, such as Geth or Parity. If you want to manage a node, you will need to familiarize yourself with the setup process for the implementation you choose to run.

Unless you want to operate a special node called an archival node, a common laptop should be sufficient to operate a full Ethereum node. At the same time, it is best not to use the device you use on a daily basis, as operating a node may slow it down significantly.

Operating a node works best on devices that can always be online. If your node goes offline, it may take a long time to synchronize with the network once back online. Hence, the best solutions are devices that are cheap to build and easy to maintain. For example, you can operate a light node on a Raspberry Pi.

## How to mine Ethereum

As the network will soon switch to Proof of Stake, mining Ethereum is not the safest long-term bet. After the transition, Ethereum miners are likely to point their mining devices to another network, or sell them in bulk.

In any case, if you want to mine Ethereum for the time being, you will need specialized hardware, such as GPU or ASIC. If you are looking for reasonable returns, you will probably need a custom mining rig and access to low-cost electricity. Additionally, you will need to create an Ethereum wallet and set up the mining software to use it. All of this requires a substantial investment of time and money, so consider it carefully before accepting the challenge.

## Ethereum's ProgPoW

ProgPoW stands for Programmatic Proof of Work. It is a proposed extension to Ethereum's mining algorithm, Ethash, designed to make GPUs more competitive with ASICs.

ASIC-resistance has been a highly debated topic for years in both the Bitcoin and Ethereum communities. In the case of Bitcoin, ASICs have become the dominant force in network mining.

On Ethereum, on the other hand, ASICs are present but much less relevant. In fact, a considerable portion of miners are still using GPUs. However, this situation may change very soon, as new companies introduce ASIC miners for Ethereum to the market. But why could ASICs be a problem?

First of all, ASICs could drastically reduce the decentralization of the network. If GPU miners are unprofitable and have to stop mining operations, the hash rate could concentrate in the hands of a handful of miners. Furthermore, developing ASIC chips is expensive, and only a few companies have the skills and resources to do it. This creates a threat of monopolization at the production level, potentially centralizing the Ethereum mining sector in the hands of a handful of corporations.

The integration of ProgPow has been a controversial topic since 2018. While some think it may be healthy for the Ethereum ecosystem, others oppose the proposal for the potential hard fork it would cause. With the transition to Proof of Stake on the way, it remains to be seen whether ProgPoW will ever be implemented on the network.

## Who develops the Ethereum software?

Like Bitcoin, Ethereum is open-source. Anyone is free to participate in the development of the protocol itself, or to build applications on top of it. In fact, Ethereum has the largest developer community in the blockchain industry.

Resources like "Mastering Ethereum" by Andreas Antonopoulos and Gavin Wood, and Developer Resources on Ethereum.org are great starting points for developers who want to participate in the development of the network.


## Solidity

Smart contracts were first described in the 1990s, but implementing them on top of blockchains posed a whole new set of challenges. Solidity was proposed in 2014 by Gavin Wood, and has since become the primary programming language for developing smart contracts on Ethereum. Syntactically, it looks like Java, JavaScript and C++.

Essentially, Solidity is what allows developers to write code that can be broken down into understandable instructions for the Ethereum Virtual Machine (EVM). If you want to learn more about how it works, Solidity's GitHub is the place to start.

It should be noted that Solidity is not the only language available to Ethereum developers. Another popular option is Vyper, which looks more like Python.

# Conclusion

Congratulations on making it to the end of this book, we hope you found some useful insights to take your cryptocurrency trading skills to the next level. As you should know by now, the world of cryptocurrency is extremely complicated and there is a new "opportunity" every way you look. However, our experience tells us that only by taking things seriously and having a proper plan you can develop your investing skills to the point that you can actually accumulate wealth.

Our final advice is to stay away from the shining objects that the world of cryptocurrencies offers you every day. Simply study the world of cryptocurrencies in depth and when you feel ready try to invest a little bit of money. Analyze your results, improve your money management skills and become the master of your emotions.

As you can see, there are no shortcuts you can take. Easy money does not exist. What exists is the possibility to start from zero and work your way up to become a professional cryptocurrency investor. The journey might be difficult, but it is certainly worth it.

# Bitcoin and Cryptocurrency

*Learn the Best Practices to Invest in the World of Blokchain in the Safest Way Possible – Discover the Power of DeFi and how it will Change the Financial System for Good!*

damages that may befall them after undertaking information described herein.

Additionally, the information in the following pages is intended only for informational purposes and should thus be thought of as universal. As befitting its nature, it is presented without assurance regarding its prolonged validity or interim quality. Trademarks that are mentioned are done without written consent and can in no way be considered an endorsement from the trademark holder.

# Table of Contents

# Introduction

Bitcoin has taken the world by storm once again when it crossed $20,000 per BTC in December of last year. After more than 2 years of bear market, the most famous cryptocurrency surpassed its previous all time high.

A lot of people are now trying to improvise themselves as professional investors and are losing a lot of money, only helping those who actually know what they are doing accumulate an incredible amount of wealth that will lead to generational fortunes.

To join the club of the few investors that actually make it, you need the right knowledge and the right mindset. Notice how we did not include a large initial capital. In fact, while having more money to invest means having more fire power, it is not necessary to have thousands of dollars to accumulate cryptocurrency and build wealth.

In fact, when we started investing in cryptocurrency we only had a few hundreds to put into the market, but that sum yielded us thousands and thousands of dollars over the span of a few years.

In this book you are going to discover everything there is to know about the fascinating world of cryptocurrency. From the operation of the Bitcoin blockchain to more advanced projects, like Uniswap and Compound.

If you diligently study the content of this book, we are sure you are going to see take your crypto knowledge to the next level. This also means you are going to see amazing results in a relative short period of time, since this bull run is offering an amazing number of opportunities.

To your success!

*Kevin Anderson*

# Chapter 1 - Cryptocurrency and Quantum Computers

With this chapter we begin our discussion of some of the potential weaknesses of the blockchain. We will show you some common scams and how to avoid them. However, before doing it we need to talk about quantum computers.

Quantum computers are powerful devices that can solve complex equations much faster than regular computers. Some experts estimate that they could crack encryption that would take today's fastest computers thousands of years just in a few minutes. As a result, much of today's digital security infrastructure would be at risk, including the cryptography behind Bitcoin and other cryptocurrencies.

## Asymmetric encryption and internet security

Asymmetric cryptography is a critical component of the cryptocurrency ecosystem and much of the internet infrastructure. It relies on a pair of keys to encrypt and decrypt information. This means that there is a public key to encrypt and a private key to decrypt. In contrast, symmetric key cryptography uses only one key to encrypt and decrypt data.

A public key can be freely shared and used to encrypt information, which can then only be decrypted by the corresponding private key. This ensures that only the chosen recipient can access the encrypted information.

One of the main benefits of asymmetric encryption is the ability to exchange information without having to share a common key over an untrusted channel. Without this fundamental capability, basic cybersecurity would not have been possible on the internet. For instance, it's hard to imagine online banking without the ability to securely encrypt information between untrusted parties.

Part of the security of asymmetric cryptography is based on the assumption that the algorithm that generates the key pair makes it incredibly difficult to calculate the private key from the public key, and at the same time keeps it simple to calculate the public key from the private key. In mathematics this model is defined as a trap door, or unidirectional function, as it is easy to calculate in one direction but difficult in the other.

Currently, most of the algorithms used to generate the key pair are based on known mathematical hash functions. These one-way functions are not known to be solvable in a feasible time frame for any existing computer. It would take an enormous amount of time for the most powerful device known to be able to perform these calculations.

However, this may soon change with the development of new computer systems called quantum computers. To understand why quantum computers are so powerful, we first need to look at how regular computers work.

## How computers work

The computers we know today can be called classical computers. This means that the calculations are performed in a sequential order. In fact, only after one computation is performed, another one can be started. This is due to the fact that the memory in a classical computer must obey the laws of physics and can only have a state of 0 or 1.

There are several hardware and software methods that allow computers to fragment complex computations into smaller chunks to gain some efficiency. However, the basis remains the same. One computation must be completed before another can be started.

Everything will be more clear with an example. Let's say a computer has to guess a 4-bit key. Each of the 4 bits can be either 0 or 1. There are 16 possible combinations.

A classic computer has to guess each combination separately, one at a time. Imagine you have a lock and 16 keys in your keychain. Each of the 16 keys must be tested separately. If the first does not open the lock, you can try the next, and so on until the right key opens the lock.

However, as the key length increases, the number of possible combinations grows exponentially. In the example we just did, adding an extra bit to increase the length to 5 bits results in 32 possible combinations. Increasing it to 6 bits results in 64 possible combinations. At 256 bits, the number of possible combinations approaches the estimated number of atoms in the observable universe.

Unfortunately, the computational processing speed only grows linearly. Doubling the processing speed of a computer only results in twice the number of attempts that can be made in a given interval. Exponential growth far exceeds any linear progress on the guessing side.

It is estimated that it would take thousands of years for a classical computational system to guess a 55-bit key. For reference, the minimum recommended size of a seed used in Bitcoin is 128 bits, and many wallet implementations use 256 bits.

It would appear that classic computers are not a threat to the asymmetric cryptography used by cryptocurrencies and the internet infrastructure.

## Quantum computers

However, there is a class of computers for which these kinds of problems would be trivial to solve. They are quantum computers. Quantum computers are based on fundamental principles described in the theory of quantum mechanics, which concerns the behavior of subatomic particles.

In classical computers, a bit is used to represent information, and a bit can have a state of 0 or 1. Quantum computers operate with quantum bits or qubits. A qubit is the basic unit of information in a quantum computer. Just like a bit, a qubit can have a state of 0 or 1. However, thanks to the peculiarity of quantum mechanical phenomena, the state of a qubit can also be 0 and 1 at the same time.

This has spurred research and development in the field of quantum computing, with universities and private companies investing time and money to explore this exciting new field. Addressing the abstract theory and practical engineering problems presented by this field is the premise of human technological breakthrough.

Unfortunately, a side effect of these quantum computers would be the trivialization of the algorithms behind asymmetric cryptography. In other words, they would practically destroy the systems that depend on it.

Let's consider the 4-bit key example again. A 4-qubit computer would theoretically be able to assume all 16 states simultaneously, in a single computation. The probability of finding the correct key would be 100% in the time it takes to perform this computation.

## Quantum-resistant encryption

The arrival of quantum computing technology could compromise the cryptography underlying much of our modern digital infrastructure, including cryptocurrencies.

This would jeopardize security, operations and communications around the world, from governments to multinational corporations to individual users. It is no surprise that a substantial amount of research is being devoted to investigating and developing countermeasures for the technology. Cryptographic algorithms that are purported to be safe against the threat of quantum computers are called quantum-resistant algorithms.

At a basic level, it appears that the risk associated with quantum computers can be mitigated with symmetric key cryptography with a simple increase in key length. This field of cryptography has been overshadowed by asymmetric key cryptography due to the problems of sharing a common secret key across an open channel. However, it could re-emerge following the development of quantum computing.

The problem of securely sharing a common key over an open channel could also find its solution in quantum cryptography itself. Progress is being made in developing countermeasures against wiretapping. Interceptors on a shared channel could be identified using the same principles necessary for the development of quantum computers. This would let you know if a shared symmetric key has previously been read or altered by a third party.

There are other research avenues being explored to counter possible quantum attacks. These may involve basic techniques such as hashing to create large message sizes. All this research is aimed at creating types of cryptography that would be difficult to decrypt even with quantum computers.

# Quantum computers and Bitcoin mining

Bitcoin mining also uses cryptography. Miners are competing to solve a cryptographic puzzle in exchange for the block reward. If a single miner had access to a quantum computer, it could achieve dominance on the network. This would reduce the decentralization of the network and expose it to a 51% attack.

However, according to some experts, this is not an immediate threat. Application-Specific Integrated Circuits (ASICs) can reduce the effectiveness of such an attack for the foreseeable future. Furthermore, if several miners have access to a quantum computer, the risk of such an attack is significantly reduced.

The development of quantum computing and the resulting threat to current implementations of asymmetric cryptography appear to be only a matter of time. However, it is not an issue of immediate concern. In fact, there are gigantic theoretical and technical hurdles to overcome before these can be fully realized.

Due to the huge stakes of cybersecurity, it makes sense to start laying the groundwork to prepare for a future attack vector. Fortunately, a great deal of research is underway into potential solutions that could be introduced into existing systems. These solutions, in theory, would be able to protect our fundamental infrastructure from the future threat of quantum computers.

Quantum-strength standards could be distributed to the general public in the same way that end-to-end encryption has been popularized across popular browsers and messaging applications. Once these standards are finalized, the cryptocurrency ecosystem could integrate the strongest possible defense against these attack vectors with relative ease.

We believe that quantum computing could represent a threat to cryptocurrency, but we also think that effective solutions will be implemented pretty fast.

# Chapter 2 - DeFi Scams

As we have seen, decentralized finance is full of innovation. It seems like a new DeFi project is launched every minute, and it's extremely difficult to keep up, let alone do the due diligence.

We often mentioned how blockchains are permissionless. Nobody needs a permit to use them, develop them or launch projects on them. While this value is a positive aspect in cryptocurrencies like Bitcoin, it also has downsides.
Anyone can launch fraudulent or deceptive projects, and there is nothing that can stop them. Well, technically, that's not quite the case. In fact, as a community we can help each other recognize some common patterns that separate legitimate innovations from misleading junk.

So what should you pay attention to? In this chapter we are going to give you some red signals that crypto scams have in common.

## What is the purpose of the project?

This might seem like an obvious question to ask, especially if you're new to DeFi.

However, most crypto assets don't introduce anything new. Of course, there are also some extremely exciting innovations. However, many new projects simply try to ride the wave of interest around DeFi without even trying to innovate.

Therefore, you should always ask yourself if the project is trying to do something new and innovative.
This is a very simple and sensible question, but by asking it you can already eliminate most of the scams.

## Development activities

Another element to consider is the activity of the developers. DeFi is closely connected to the open-source ethos.
If you have any programming knowledge, you can take a look at the code directly. Being open-source, if the project attracts enough interest there will surely be other people doing it. This can probably reveal if the project has bad intentions or not.

In addition to this, you can also observe the development activity. Are developers continuing to implement new code? While this parameter may be faked, it is still a good indicator to find out if the developers are serious about it or are just trying to make a quick buck.

## Audit of smart contracts

In the context of smart contracts and DeFi, we often talk about audits. These are control processes with the aim of making sure that the code is secure. While an essential part of smart contract development, many developers implement their code without any audits. This can greatly increase the risk associated with the use of these contracts.

One thing to note is that audits are expensive. Legitimate projects usually manage to pay for them, but fraudulent projects don't use them in order to save money.

Does this mean that if a project has had an audit is completely safe to use? No. Audits are required, but no audits will ensure total security. Always be aware of the associated risks when depositing your funds into a smart contract.

## Are the founders anonymous?

The crypto world is deeply rooted in the freedom of anonymity that the internet can provide. After all, we will probably never find out the identity of Satoshi Nakamoto.

However, teams with anonymous founders still represent an additional risk to consider. If they turn out to be scammers, there's a good chance they can't account for their crimes. While on-chain analytics tools are becoming increasingly sophisticated, the situation is different if founders stake their real-world reputation for identity.

Remember that not all projects run by anonymous teams are scams. There are undoubtedly many examples of legitimate projects with anonymous teams. However, you should take into account the implications of an anonymous team when evaluating projects.

## Tokens distribution

Token economics is a crucial aspect of the research on a DeFi project. One of the ways a scammer can make money is to pump up the price of the token and then sell its large reserves on the market.

What if, for example, 40-50-60% of the outstanding offer is sold on the open market? The price of the token collapses, losing almost all of its value. While a meaningful allocation to the founder is not considered a wake-up call in itself, it can lead to problems in the future.

In addition to allocations, you need to consider how tokens are distributed. Is it an Initial Coin Offering (ICO)? Or an Initial Exchange Offering (IEO) in which a cryptocurrency exchange puts its reputation on the line? Are they distributing tokens via an airdrop that is likely to cause severe sales pressure?

Token distribution models have a lot of nuances to consider. In many cases, it is even difficult to find this information, which is alarming in itself. However, if you want to get a complete picture of the project, they are absolutely essential data.

## How likely is an exit scam?

Yield farming is a new method used to launch DeFi tokens. Many new DeFi projects use this distribution model. The idea is that users block their funds in smart contracts and receive a portion of the new tokens issued in exchange.

Maybe you understand where we want to go. Some projects simply take funds from the liquidity pool. Others take more sophisticated methods, or have a huge pre-mine process that dilutes the supply to infinity.

Additionally, new altcoins are often listed on automated market makers such as Uniswap or Sushiswap before making it to regular exchanges. If the project team is providing much of the liquidity for the market pair on the AMM, they could simply remove it and sell the tokens on the market. Typically this pushes the token price down to zero. Since there is no market to sell to anymore, the event is often called a rug pull.

If you want to take part in the wild west of yield farming or just use decentralized protocols to trade and invest, DeFi scams are a considerable risk. We hope these general guidelines can help you better recognize fraudulent and malicious projects.

When in doubt, do not invest. There are thousands of good projects, do not let fear of missing out guide your decisions.

# Chapter 3 - Cryptocurrency Scams and Mobile Phones

2020 was an extraordinary year for the cryptocurrency industry, thanks to the rapid increase in valuations that catapulted them into the mainstream media. Predictably, this aroused enormous interest from both the general public and cybercriminals. The relative anonymity offered by cryptocurrencies has made them a very popular tool among criminals who often use them to bypass traditional banking systems and avoid financial control by regulators.

Considering that on average more time is spent on smartphones than on computers, it is not surprising that cybercriminals have also turned their attention to mobile phones. The next few pages highlight the ways scammers are targeting cryptocurrency users via their mobile devices, along with some steps you can take to protect yourself.

## Fake cryptocurrency exchange apps

The best known example of a fake cryptocurrency exchange app is probably the case of Poloniex. Prior to the launch of their official mobile trading app in July 2018, Google Play already had a list of numerous bogus apps claiming to be the Poloniex exchange, intentionally designed to be a scam. Several users who downloaded these fraudulent apps saw their login credentials compromised, and their cryptocurrencies stolen. Some apps even required access credentials to the user's Gmail account. It is important to point out that only accounts without two-factor authentication were compromised.

There are measures that can help protect you from such scams. Here is what you need to do every time you download an exchange app.

- Check the official website of the exchange to see if there really is a mobile trading app. If so, use the link on the site.

- Read reviews and check ratings. Fraudulent apps often have several negative reviews and people complaining that they have been scammed, so be sure to take a look before downloading. However, you should also be skeptical of apps that feature perfect ratings and comments. Any legitimate app has its fair share of negative reviews.

- Check the app developer information. See if a legitimate website, email address, and name are provided. Do an online search for this information to see if it is really linked to the official exchange.

- Check the number of downloads. The download count must always be considered. A heavily used cryptocurrency exchange is unlikely to have a low number of downloads.

- Activate 2FA on your accounts. While not 100% secure, 2FA is much more difficult to bypass and can make a huge difference in protecting your funds, even if your login credentials are stolen.

## Fake cryptocurrency wallet apps

There are many different types of fraudulent apps. One type of these apps seeks to obtain personal information such as passwords and private wallet keys.

In some cases, fake apps provide users with previously generated public addresses. This way, they believe that the funds are deposited in these addresses. However, they do not have the private keys and consequently cannot access the funds sent to them.

Fake wallets of this type have been created for popular cryptocurrencies such as Ethereum and Neo. Sadly many users have lost their funds.

The precautions described in the segment on exchange apps are also applicable in this case. However, an additional precaution to take when it comes to app wallets is to make sure that new addresses are generated when the app is first opened, and that you are in possession of the private keys. A legitimate wallet app allows you to export private keys, but it's also important to make sure the generation of new key pairs isn't compromised.

Even if the app provides a private key, you should check if public addresses are accessible from it. For example, some Bitcoin wallets allow users to import their own private keys or seeds to view addresses and access funds. To minimize the risk of key or seed damage, you can perform this process on a computer that is not connected to the internet.

## Cryptojacking apps

Cryptojacking is widely used by cybercriminals due to low barriers to entry and rather low overall costs. Plus, it offers the potential for a steady long-term income. Despite having less computing power than PCs, mobile devices are increasingly becoming a target of cryptojacking.

In addition to cryptojacking on web browsers, cybercriminals are developing programs that appear to be legitimate games, utilities or education apps. However, many of them are designed to secretly run crypto-mining scripts in the background.

There are also cryptojacking apps that are advertised as legitimate third-party miners, but the rewards are sent to the developer instead of the users. Complicating the situation is the fact that criminals have become increasingly sophisticated, employing light mining algorithms to avoid detection.

Cryptojacking is incredibly bad for your mobile devices, as it degrades performance and accelerates deterioration. It could act as a Trojan for worse malware.

In order to defend yourself from cryptojacking, only download apps from official stores, such as Google Play. The pirated apps have not been checked and are more likely to contain cryptojacking scripts.

Check your smartphone for excessive overheating or battery drain apps. Once detected, terminate the apps that are causing the issue.
Use a web browser that protects against cryptojacking or install reliable browser plug-ins, such as MinerBlock, NoCoin, and

AdBlock. Furthermore, if possible, install mobile antivirus software and keep it up to date.

## App for giveaways and fake crypto-miners

These are apps that pretend to be mining cryptocurrencies for their users when they actually do nothing other than display advertisements. They encourage users to keep the app open by showing a gradual increase in rewards over time. Some apps incentivize users to leave 5-star ratings to receive rewards. Of course, none of these apps are actually mining, and users never get the advertised rewards.

To protect yourself from these scams, you need to keep in mind that for the vast majority of cryptocurrencies, mining requires highly specialized hardware (ASICs). This means that mining on a mobile device is not possible. The amount you would be able to get would be insignificant, if not non-existent. Stay away from this type of app.

## Clipper app

These apps modify the addresses copy by replacing them with those of the attacker. Therefore, even if the victim copies the correct recipient address, the one they paste to process the transaction is replaced by one owned by the attacker.

In order not to fall victim to such apps, always check and double check the address you are pasting in the recipient field. Blockchain transactions are irreversible, so be very careful. It is best to check the entire address, not just the parts. Some apps are smart enough to paste addresses that look similar to the original address.

## SIM swapping

In a scam involving SIM swapping, a criminal gains access to a user's phone number, typically through social engineering techniques to trick telephone operators into sending a new SIM card. The best-known SIM swapping scam hit cryptocurrency entrepreneur Michael Terpin. According to claims, AT&T has been negligent in handling its mobile credentials, leading to the loss of tokens worth USD 20 million.

Once the cybercriminals have gained access to your phone number, they can use it to bypass any 2FA associated with it. At this point, they can access wallets and accounts on cryptocurrency exchanges.

Another method employed by cybercriminals is the monitoring of SMS communications. Weak spots in communication networks can allow criminals to intercept messages that may contain authentication codes. What makes this attack particularly troubling is the fact that users are not required to take any action, such as downloading bogus software or clicking a malicious link.

Do not use your mobile number for 2FA via SMS. Instead, use apps like Google Authenticator or Authy to protect your accounts. Cybercriminals cannot access these apps even if they get hold of your phone number. Alternatively, you can use 2FA hardware like YubiKey or Google's Titan Security Key. Do not disclose personal information, such as your phone number, on social media. Cybercriminals can collect this information and use it to impersonate you somewhere else.

Claiming to own cryptocurrencies on social media means becoming a target. If you find yourself in a position where everyone already knows you hold some crypto, avoid revealing personal information, including the exchanges or wallets you use.

Make arrangements for your mobile operator to protect your account. This can mean associating a code or password to your account and indicating that only users who know the code can make changes. Alternatively, you can request that these changes are only possible in person and not allow them over the phone.

## Wifi

Cybercriminals are constantly looking for access points to mobile devices, especially those in the hands of cryptocurrency users. One of these access points is WiFi. Public WiFi networks are not secure and precautions must be taken before connecting to them. Otherwise, you risk discovering a weakness that attackers can exploit to access data on mobile devices.

Mobile phones have become an essential part of our lives. In fact, they are so intertwined with the user's digital identity that they become its greatest vulnerability. Cybercriminals know this very well and will continue to find new ways to take advantage of it. Protecting your mobile devices is no longer optional. It has become a necessity. Watch out.

# Chapter 4 - More on Cryptojacking

Cryptojacking is a cyber attack in which an infected device is secretly exploited for cryptocurrency mining. The hacker uses the victims' computing power and broadband. Typically, the crypto mining malware responsible for these activities is designed to use limited resources, so as to remain undisturbed for as long as possible. Since cryptocurrency mining requires a lot of computing power, hackers try to infect a large number of devices. By doing so, they are able to obtain sufficient computational resources for low-risk, low-cost mining.

Previous versions of mining malware kicked in when victims clicked on malicious links or email attachments, infecting their system with a hidden crypto-miner. However, over the past two years, more sophisticated types have been developed, taking the cryptojacking approach to a whole new level. Currently, much of the mining malware operates through scripts implemented within websites. This approach is known as web-based cryptojacking.

## Web-based cryptojacking

Web-based cryptojacking is the most common form of crypto mining malware. Typically, this attack is performed through scripts running within a website, to force the victim's browser to mine cryptocurrencies automatically for the entire duration of the visit. These web-based miners are secretly being introduced to a wide range of websites, regardless of popularity or category. In most cases, Monero is the cryptocurrency of choice, as the mining process does not require large amounts of resources and computing power like Bitcoin mining. In addition, Monero guarantees a greater level of privacy and anonymity, making transactions much more difficult to trace.

Unlike ransomware, cryptomining malware almost never compromises your computer and the data on it. The most obvious effect of cryptojacking is the reduction in CPU performance. For businesses and large organizations, low CPU performance can hinder business, resulting in potential huge losses and missed opportunities.

## CoinHive

The web-based approach to cryptojacking made its appearance in September 2017, with the public launch of a crypto-miner called CoinHive. This program is a JavaScript crypto-miner apparently created for a good cause. In fact, it allows website owners to monetize their free content without having to depend on unsavory advertisements.

CoinHive is compatible with all popular browsers and is relatively easy to use. Creators receive 30% of all mined cryptocurrencies through the code. The remaining 70% is distributed to user accounts identified through cryptographic keys.

Despite being presented as an interesting tool, CoinHive has received a lot of criticism as it is currently being used by hackers to secretly smuggle the miner into several infected websites (without the owner's permission).

In the few cases where CoinHive is intentionally implemented for good reasons, the cryptojacking JavaScript is configured in an Opt-In version called AuthedMine, a modified version that starts mining only after receiving the visitor's consent.

Unsurprisingly, AuthedMine hasn't spread as widely as CoinHive. A quick search on PublicWWW shows that there are at least 14,900 websites using CoinHive. On the other hand, AuthedMine was implemented by approximately 1,250 pages.

In 2018, CoinHive became the leading malware threat monitored by anti-virus programs and cybersecurity companies.

However, recent reports indicate that cryptojacking is no longer the most prevalent threat, as the first and second positions are currently occupied by banking Trojans and Ransomware attacks.

The rapid decline of cryptojacking could be linked to the work of cybersecurity companies, as several cryptojacking codes have been blacklisted and quickly detected by most anti-virus software. Furthermore, recent analysis suggests that web-based cryptojacking is not as profitable as it seems.

## Examples of cryptojacking

In December 2017, the CoinHive code was secretly implemented in the WiFi network of several Buenos Aires Starbucks, as reported by a customer. The script used the computing power of any connected device for Monero mining.

In early 2018, the CoinHive miner was identified within Youtube Ads, running through Google's DoubleClick platform. In July and August 2018, a cryptojacking attack infected more than 200,000 MikroTik routers in Brazil, injecting the CoinHive code into a huge amount of web traffic.

## How to identify and prevent cryptojacking attacks

If you suspect that your CPU is being used more than usual and the cooling fans are making noise for no reason, it is likely that your device is being used for crypto mining. It is important to find out if your computer is infected or if cryptojacking is taking place on the browser. Web-based cryptojacking is relatively simple to detect and stop. On the contrary, mining malware that target computer systems and networks are not always easy to find, as they have been developed to remain hidden or disguised as something legitimate.

There are browser extensions that can effectively prevent most web-based cryptojacking attacks. However, in addition to being limited to web-based miners, these countermeasures are usually on a static blacklist, which may soon become obsolete with the arrival of new types of attacks. Therefore, it is also recommended to keep your operating system and anti-virus software up to date.

In the case of businesses and large organizations, it is important to inform and educate employees about cryptojacking and phishing techniques, such as fraudulent emails and spoofing websites.

# Chapter 5 - Dusting Attacks

The term dusting attack refers to a new form of attack in which hackers and scammers try to break the privacy of Bitcoin and other cryptocurrency users by sending minimal amounts of coins to their personal wallets. Several users act on the assumption that their anonymity is well protected from attempts to infiltrate their transactions, but unfortunately this is not the case.

## Definition of dust

When it comes to cryptocurrency, the term dust refers to small amounts of a coin or token. This is an amount so small that it is almost always ignored. Taking Bitcoin as an example, the smallest unit of currency is 1 satoshi (0.00000001 BTC) and we can define dust as a couple of hundred satoshis.

In other words, the dust is a tiny amount that is not worth sending, as it is much less than the cost of the transaction itself. Within cryptocurrency exchanges, dust also indicates the tiny amounts of coins that "remain stuck" and cannot be sold.

Almost no one pays attention to the dust in their wallet and rarely cares about its origins. Until recently, these minimal amounts could be ignored without problems, but with the creation of dusting attacks, things have changed.

## Dusting attacks

The scammers found that Bitcoin users don't pay much attention to these small amounts in their wallets, so they started dusting a large number of addresses by sending them a few satoshis. They monitored those funds and all targeted wallet transactions, managing to link and eventually determine the companies or individuals behind those addresses. Dusting attacks started with Bitcoin but currently happen with other cryptocurrencies operating on a public and transparent blockchain.

At the end of October 2018, the developers of Samourai Wallet, a wallet for Bitcoin, announced that some users have been victims of dusting attacks. The company posted a tweet warning and explaining to everyone how to protect themselves. To defend its users from dusting attacks, the wallet offers a real-time dust tracking alarm and a "Do Not Spend" feature that allows users to mark suspicious funds and prevent them from being used in future transactions.

If a dust is not moved, hackers are unable to trace the connections they need to "de-anonymize" the users of the wallet or the owner of the address. Samourai wallet already offers the possibility to automatically report transactions below the limit of 564 satoshi. This is a feature that guarantees a certain level of protection.

## The Pseudonymity of Bitcoin

Since Bitcoin is public and decentralized, anyone can create a wallet and join the network without providing personal information. Although all bitcoin transactions are public and visible, it is not always easy to find the identity behind an address or a transaction. For this reason Bitcoin is quite private, but not entirely.

Peer-to-peer transactions, i.e. transactions made between two parties without the involvement of an intermediary, are more likely to remain anonymous. It should be noted that Bitcoin users should use each address only once, in order to preserve their privacy.

However, most traders and investors use exchange platforms and will eventually end up having their own personal wallets linked to wallets on exchanges. Therefore, if you are a cryptocurrency trader, it is important to choose a safe and reliable exchange.

It is important to keep in mind that, unlike the opinion of many, Bitcoin is not an anonymous cryptocurrency. In addition to the recently created dusting attacks, there are several research laboratories, companies and government agencies that carry out analysis on the blockchain to de-anonymize it.

## Other privacy and security issues

Even though the Bitcoin blockchain is nearly impossible to attack, wallets are a weak link in this chain. Since users don't provide personal information when they create an account, they can't prove a theft in case a hacker gets access to their coins. Furthermore, even if they could, it would still be useless.

In fact, trying to investigate a bitcoin theft is a useless undertaking for the victims. If you own bitcoins in a personal wallet, which only you can access, you are acting as a personal bank and there is nothing you can do if you lose your keys or if your coins are stolen.

Privacy becomes more valuable every day. Not just for those who have something to hide but for all of us. It is even more valuable for cryptocurrency traders and investors. In addition to dusting attacks and other attacks of a similar nature, you need to be wary of other rapidly evolving threats in the field of cryptocurrencies, such as Cryptojacking, Ransomware, and

Phishing. Additionally, you should consider using a VPN along with a reputable antivirus program on all of your devices. Protect your wallets and store your keys in encrypted folders.

# Chapter 6 - Other Common Cryptocurrency Scams

In today's world, your cryptocurrencies are an incredibly valuable asset to criminals. They are liquid, highly portable, and once a transaction is made, it is virtually impossible to reverse it. As a result, a wave of scams has engulfed the digital world.

In this chapter, we will explain some of the most common crypto scams.

## Social media giveaway scams

It's amazing how everyone seems so generous on Twitter and Facebook. Take a look at the comments of a tweet with high engagement and you will surely see that one of your favorite crypto companies or influencers is doing a giveaway. If you only send 1 BNB / BTC / ETH, they promise to send you 10x this amount back. Sounds too good to be true, right? Unfortunately, that's because that's not true.

It is incredibly unlikely that anyone organizing a legitimate giveaway requests money. On social media, you should be wary of these types of messages. They might come from accounts that look identical to the ones you know and follow, but that's part of the trick.

Of course, you should just ignore them. If you are really convinced that they are legitimate, check the profiles and you will see the differences. You will quickly realize that the Twitter handle or Facebook profile is fake.

And even if Binance or other entities decide to organize a giveaway, they will never ask you to send funds first.

## Pyramid and Ponzi schemes

Pyramid and Ponzi schemes are slightly different, but we put them in the same category for their similarities. Either way, the scam is based on a participant bringing in new members with the promise of incredible earnings.

## Ponzi schemes

In a Ponzi scheme, you may hear about a guaranteed profit investment opportunity. Typically, you will see the scheme disguised as a portfolio management service. In reality, there is no magic formula. The "returns" received are only other investors' money.

The organizer will take an investor's money and add it to a pool. The only money flowing into the pool comes from newcomers. Older investors are paid with the money of the newest investors, a cycle that can continue as new participants join. The scam collapses when there is no more money coming in.

Consider, for example, a service that promises a 10% return in one month. You could contribute $100. The organizer then convinces another 'customer', and they too invest $100. Using this newly acquired money, the organizer can pay you the $110 at the end of the month. Later they will have to lure another customer in order to pay the second one and so on. The cycle continues until the inevitable implosion of the scheme.

## Pyramid schemes

In a pyramid scheme, there is a little more work to do for those involved. At the top of the pyramid is the organizer. This character will recruit a certain number of people to work in the level below them, and each of these people will recruit a number of people, etc. The result is a huge structure that grows exponentially and branches out as new levels are created.

So far, we've only described the graph of a very large business. But a pyramid scheme stands out in that it promises returns for recruiting new members. Let's make an example. The organizer gives Alice and Bob the right to recruit new members for $100 each, and takes a 50% share on their subsequent returns. Alice and Bob can offer the same deal to those they recruit.

If Alice sells memberships to Carol and Dan for $ 100 each, she will have $100 left over because half of the profits must be sent to the level above her. If Carol later sells memberships, Alice will see the profits go up. In fact, Alice gets half of Carol's profits, and the organizer gets half of Alice's half.

As the pyramid scheme grows, older members generate an increasing revenue stream due to distribution costs moving from lower to higher tiers. However, due to exponential growth, the model is not sustainable for long. Sometimes, participants pay for the rights to sell a product or service. You may have heard of some multi-level marketing companies accused of organizing pyramid schemes in this way.

In the context of blockchain and cryptocurrencies, controversial projects like OneCoin, Bitconnect and PlusToken have come under fire, with users engaging in legal action against them for allegedly operating pyramid schemes.

## Phishing

Even newcomers to the crypto field will surely be familiar with the practice of phishing. It usually consists of the scammer impersonating a person or company to obtain personal data from victims. It can happen through many means - phone, email, fake websites or messaging apps. Messaging app scams are particularly common in the context of cryptocurrencies.

There is no single protocol used by scammers to try to obtain personal information. You may receive emails alerting you to something wrong with your exchange account, prompting you to follow a link to resolve the issue. This link will redirect you to a bogus website which will ask you to log in. This way, the hacker will steal your credentials, and possibly your cryptocurrencies.

A common scam on Telegram sees the scammer prowl around official crypto wallet or exchange groups. When a user reports a problem in the group, the scammer contacts the user in private, impersonating customer support or team members. At this point, they will ask the user to share their personal information and the seed phrase.

If someone finds out about your seed phrase, they will have access to your funds. You must not disclose it to anyone, under any circumstances, not even to legitimate companies. Wallet troubleshooting does not require knowledge of your seed, so you can assume that anyone who asks you for it is a scammer.

As for exchange accounts, they will never ask you for your password. The most prudent course of action when receiving an unsolicited communication is to not respond, and to contact the company via the contact details indicated on their official website.

## Personal returns

The term DYOR - Do Your Own Research - is often repeated in the cryptocurrency field, and for a very good reason.

When it comes to investing, you should never take anyone's word for granted about which cryptocurrencies or tokens to buy. You never know what their true intentions are. They might get paid to promote a particular ICO or have a large personal investment. This applies to both random people and renowned influencers and personalities. No project has a guarantee of success. In fact, many will fail.

To be able to evaluate a project objectively, you should consider a combination of factors. Everyone has a different approach when it comes to finding potential investments. Here are some general questions to get you started.

- How were the coins / tokens distributed?
- Is most of the supply concentrated in the hands of a few entities?

- What is the unique highlight of this particular project?
- What other projects are doing the same thing, and why is this superior?
- Who is working on the project? Does the team have a strong track record?
- How is the community? What are they building?
- Does the world really need this coin / token?

The bad guys are never short of techniques to steal funds from unsuspecting cryptocurrency users. To stay away from the most common scams, you must constantly remain alert and aware of the patterns used by these characters. Always try to use official websites or applications, and remember: if an investment sounds too good to be true, it probably is.

# Chapter 7 - More on Cryptocurrency Phishing

Generally speaking phishing is a type of cyber attack in which a hacker pretends to be an entity or company with a proven reputation in order to deceive its victims and obtain sensitive information about it. This information can include credit card details, usernames, passwords, and so on. Since phishing involves psychological manipulation and is based on human error, it is considered a social engineering attack.

Typically, phishing attacks use fraudulent emails that convince the user to enter sensitive information on a compromised website. These emails usually ask you to reset your password or confirm your credit card information, redirecting to fake websites that look very similar to the originals. The main types of phishing are clone phishing, spear phishing and pharming.

Phishing attacks are also used in the cryptocurrency ecosystem, where hackers try to steal Bitcoin or other digital currencies from users. One of the methods applied consists in spoofing a real website and changing its wallet address to that of the hacker, making users believe that they are paying for a legitimate service. However, in reality their money ends up in the wrong pockets.

## Different types of phishing

There are different types of phishing, classified according to the target and attack vector. Here is a list of the most common examples.

- Clone phishing. In this case a hacker uses a legitimate e-mail sent previously, copying its contents to create a similar one containing a link to a compromised site. The hacker could also add that this link is the updated version, perhaps stating that the previous one has expired.

- Spear phishing. This type of attack targets a single person or entity (usually someone famous) by collecting and using identifiable information, such as the name of a relative or friend.

- Pharming. In this case, the hacker modifies a DNS record which, in practice, redirects visitors to a legitimate website to a previously compromised one. This is the most dangerous of the attacks as the DNS records are not under the control of the user, thus rendering them defenseless.

- Whaling. This is a form of spear phishing that targets wealthy and important people, such as CEOs and government officials.

- Email spoofing. Phishing emails typically copy communications from legitimate companies or people. Such emails can present unsuspecting victims with links to compromised sites, where hackers collect login credentials using cleverly disguised login pages. Pages may contain Trojans, keyloggers, and other malicious scripts that steal personal information.

- Redirects. Redirects lead users to URLs other than the ones they intend to visit. Hackers can exploit vulnerabilities by injecting redirects and installing malware on users' computers.

- Typosquatting. Typosquatting directs web traffic to forge websites that use spelling in another language, common mistakes or subtle variations of high-level domains. Phishers use these domains to mimic the interfaces of legitimate sites, taking advantage of users who misspell the URL.

- The 'Watering Hole'. In a watering hole attack, phishers track users' profiles and determine which websites they visit the most. They then scan these sites for vulnerabilities and, if possible, insert malicious scripts designed to target users the next time they visit the site.

- Impersonation and giveaways. Another technique used in phishing schemes includes impersonating influential people on social media. Phishers could impersonate important members of companies and, depending on the target audience, can promote giveaways or other deceptive practices. Victims of these tricks can also be individually targeted via social engineering processes aimed at finding naive users. Hackers could attack verified accounts and change their usernames to impersonate a real person, while maintaining the verified status. Victims tend to provide their credentials and interact more with influential people, giving phishers the opportunity to leverage the information they collect.

Recently, phishers have started targeting platforms like Slack, Discord, and Telegram. Beware if you use those apps on a regular basis.

- Advertising. Advertising is another tactic used for phishing. Fake ads can use typosquatting domains, as well as pay to make them more visible in search results. The sites may also appear as the first search result for legitimate companies or services. These sites are often used as a means of stealing sensitive information, including login credentials to your trading accounts.

- Malicious applications. Phishers can also use infected apps as a vector to inject malware that monitors your behavior or steals personal information. Apps can appear as price trackers, wallets, and other crypto-related tools.

- Text and voice phishing. Text and voice phishing are other means used by hackers to collect personal information.

## Phishing vs Pharming

While pharming is considered by some to be a type of phishing attack, it is based on a different mechanism. The central difference between phishing and pharming is the fact that phishing requires the victim to make a mistake, whereas pharming only needs the victim to try to access a legitimate website with a hacked DNS record.

## Preventing phishing

Here are a few tips you can follow to stay away from phishing attacks.

- Be cautious. The best defense against phishing is to think critically about the emails you receive. Did you expect to receive an email from someone regarding that topic? Do you suspect that the information that person is looking for is not linked to the subject of the e-mail? If you have any doubts, try your best to contact the sender through different means.

- Check the content. You can copy part of the content or the sender's e-mail address into a search engine to check for traces of phishing attacks that used that specific method.

- Try other ways. If you believe you have received a legitimate request to confirm your account credentials for an activity you know, try to do it through different ways instead of clicking the link in the email.

- Check the URL. Hover the mouse over the link, without clicking, to check if it starts with HTTPS and not HTTP. However, remember that this element alone does not guarantee that the site is legitimate.

- Never share your private keys. Do not send the private key of your Bitcoin wallet to anyone, and verify that the seller you are about to send cryptocurrencies to is legitimate. The difference in using crypto instead of credit cards is that there is no central authority to resolve a dispute in the event that you do not receive the agreed product or service. For this reason it is always necessary to be extremely careful when dealing with cryptocurrency transactions.

If you follow these tips, you will not have any issues. Just be careful and everything will be fine.

# Chapter 8 - Cryptocurrency and Keyloggers

A keylogger is a tool designed to capture all keystrokes on a computer, through a software program or hardware device. This keyboard logging activity is also called keylogging or keystroke logging.

While keyloggers are not illegal, their use is often linked to illegal operations.

## Positive uses of a keylogger

Even if they are used mainly for illegal activities, keyloggers have some positive use cases. They can help parents monitor what their children are doing, and offer employers a tool to monitor how employees use computers during their working hours. It should be noted, however, that this must be done with the consent of the employees. A keylogger can also be used to protect passwords and other data in the event of a computer failure. Furthermore, keystroke logging has recently been adopted by scientists and established as a research tool in the study of human writing processes.

## Negative uses of a keylogger

As the name suggests, the purpose of a keylogger is to record every single keystroke from a computer, which in itself is not necessarily a bad thing. Unfortunately, however, the most common use of keyloggers is linked to illegal activities. Keylogging programs are widely used by cybercriminals as a means of stealing sensitive information, such as exchange login credentials, passwords, personal emails, wallet credentials, driver's license numbers, and so on.

## Types of Keyloggers

As mentioned earlier, there are two main types of keylogging devices. The software version and the hardware version.

## Preventing the installation of a hardware keylogger

It is highly unlikely to fall victim to a hardware keylogger, especially in the privacy of your home. However, it is possible in a public setting. Since a hardware keylogger typically uses a USB input, the best defense is to regularly check all inputs on the computer you are using.

When writing sensitive information, such as a password, you can also use the mouse to confuse a possible keylogger. For example, writing the last character of the password first and moving the cursor to write the rest. The keylogger will record the last character as the first. Selecting and replacing text as you type is another option. You can test several variations of these deceptive typing techniques. However, they are not very practical and may not be enough for sophisticated keyloggers, such as those that also record screen or mouse activity.

## How to identify and remove a software keylogger

The easiest way to detect a keylogger software is to check running programs in the system process window. If there is something that seems odd, an online search should be enough to find out whether it is a legitimate program or a known keylogger. Furthermore, analyzing the traffic leaving your computer is another good idea.

Removing a keylogger software is not easy but it is possible. The first thing to do is to install an anti-keylogger program and check if it can be deleted. If your computer keeps doing strange things and you suspect that the anti-keylogger program was unable to fix the problem, you should probably format and reinstall your operating system.

# Chapter 9 - How to Protect Your Binance Account

In the previous chapters we have described some of the most common scams in the cryptocurrency space. One important security aspect to keep in mind is the safety of your exchange account. Since we recommend Binance, this chapter will be tailored to this exchange. However, you can apply the same principle to the platform of your choice.

## Use a strong password and change it regularly

This may sound pretty obvious, but it is a vital step in securing your Binance account. You should use strong and unique passwords for each of your Internet accounts. This is especially true for those that contain value. Ideally, these passwords should be more than 8 characters, including upper and lower case letters, numbers and special characters.

One of the best ways to generate, manage and store secure passwords are password managers. This way, you can safely and conveniently store and manage your various passwords, all in the same place. Most password managers use sophisticated encryption mechanisms to provide an additional layer of security. Make sure you only use a reputable password manager software and create a strong master password.

Having a strong password is an excellent first step, but it doesn't mean you're good to go forever. It is good practice to change your passwords on a regular basis, as hackers may still be able to get your passwords. This not only applies to your Binance account, but also to the email associated with your Binance account.

Speaking of email, here's another factor to consider. It's helpful to use different email addresses for different accounts. This way, you can mitigate some of the potentially damaging effects of data breaches. Especially if you're using an old email account, there's a good chance it has been part of a breach in the past. However, if you're using dedicated email addresses for each service, the odds of a breach affecting multiple accounts are lower. The "Have I Been Pwned" website is a great resource for checking if any of your accounts have ever been the victim of a data breach.

Remember that when you change your Binance account password, you will not be able to withdraw funds for the next 24 hours. This measure is to prevent potential hackers from locking you out of your account while withdrawing your funds.

## Enable Two-Factor Authentication

Enabling Two-Factor Authentication (2FA) should be one of the first things to do after creating a Binance account. Binance supports two types of 2FA: SMS and Google Authenticator. Of these two, we recommend Google Authenticator. Make sure you write down your recovery key so that you can transfer your 2FA codes to a new phone in case you need to.

While SMS authentication may be easier to use, it is considered less secure than Google Authenticator. SIM swapping is a real threat, and some high-profile accounts have fallen victim to this technique. In 2019, Twitter CEO Jack Dorsey was attacked with this method, leaving hackers full power over his Twitter account with millions of followers.

These aren't the only ways to protect your account with 2FA. We'll talk about another method called Universal 2nd Factor authentication shortly. It is a secure hardware device that protects your account. And, good news, Binance supports this too.

## Check the list of devices authorized to access your account

You can check the devices that are allowed to access your Binance account in the Device Management tab. When using the Binance app, you can find this tab in the "Account" section.

If you see devices you don't recognize or use anymore, delete them. Once a device is removed, it will no longer be able to access your account, unless you authorize it again via the confirmation email. As we discussed earlier, this is why the security of your email account is of paramount importance.

You can check account activity, i.e. from which IP address your account was used and when. If you see anything suspicious, immediately deactivate your account. This will suspend trading and withdrawals, delete all your API keys and remove all devices that can access your account.

## Manage your withdrawal addresses

Your Binance account has a security feature called Address Management. It allows you to limit the wallet addresses to which you can withdraw funds. If you activate it, any new addresses you add will require an email confirmation to be whitelisted.

Again, this is why keeping your email account safe is so important. It is the foundation of your online security.

## Learn more about phishing

Phishing is a type of attack in which an attacker tries to impersonate someone else with the aim of obtaining your personal information. This is one of the most common attacks out there, so you should be very cautious.

As a general rule, it's best to only visit Binance from a saved bookmark instead of typing the address every time. With this simple step, you can already avoid a good portion of the fake Binance sites trying to trick you into stealing your account information.

The Anti-Phishing Code feature allows you to set a unique code to include in all your Binance notification emails. By activating the Anti-Phishing Code, you will be able to check if the emails you receive from Binance are genuine.

## Follow the API security guidelines

Binance API is a great way for more advanced traders to maximize their experience with the Binance trading engine. Binance API allows you to create custom trading strategies.

However, using API keys comes with some risks, as you are allowing your data to be shared with external applications.

When using the Binance API, you should consider restricting access based on IP address. This way, only the IP addresses in the whitelist can be activated. You should also consider changing your API keys on a regular basis, and avoid giving your keys to outside parties.

## Use Universal 2nd Factor authentication

Binance supports U2F compatible authenticators, such as Yubico's YubiKey. These devices will only allow you to log into your account if they are connected to your computer or paired wirelessly.

You can think of this device as a system similar to your Google Authenticator, with the difference that, instead of software, it is hardware. This means that logging into your account also requires physical access to this hardware.

We encourage to check out YubiKey if you are leaving significant amounts on Binance. However, always keep in mind that the only way to truly protect your funds is to keep them in a cold wallet.

# Chapter 10 - Crypto and Passive Income: Binance Lending

In the next few chapters we are going to take a look at some ways to earn passive income on your cryptocurrencies. We have mentioned some DeFi options earlier in this book. However, centralized alternatives are easier to use for the average Joe and provide a greater degree of security if you are just starting out.

Whether you are a holder or a crypto trader, you have several choices to earn passive income with your funds. One of these is the granting of loans. This process is incredibly easy to do on Binance. What makes loans very convenient is their ability to make you earn regardless of the general market trend.

In this chapter, we will discuss how Binance Lending works, which types of loan products can you choose and how to make your funds work for you.

## An overview of Binance Lending

Binance Lending allows you to easily grow your capital accumulating interest on your funds. Essentially, you are lending your assets to traders with margin on the platform, which pay you interests to borrow your funds. You can choose from a wide range of options, including Bitcoin, Ethereum, Binance USD, Tether and many others.

There are two types of binance lending loan products: fixed deposits and flexible deposits. Fixed deposits allow you to block your funds for a time interval at a predetermined interest. On the contrary, flexible deposits allow you to withdraw your funds at any time, and the interest rate changes over time. Having the flexibility to access your funds, interest rates will be lower for flexible deposits products.

Interests are distributed every day for flexible deposits, or at the withdraw date for fixed deposits.

## How to use Binance Lending

Using Binance Lending is very simple. Here is how to do it.

- Access your Binance account. If you don't have one yet, register and create it. It only takes a few minutes.
- Click on lending;
- Click on products;
- Select the type of loan product you want to use: flexible deposits or fixed deposits.
- Select the coin you want to earn interests on and you are ready to go.

We remind you that the BNBs you subscribe to for any product of Binance lending will continue to count in snapshot calculations for the Binance launchpad. This means that you can participate in the Initial Exchange Offers (IEO) and at the same time earn interest on your funds!

## Fixed deposits

A fixed-deposit loan product involves the lock of your funds for a period of time at a predetermined interest. This option is more suited to long-term investors, who want to hold their crypto for the long term.

Keep in mind that if you lock your crypto to a fixed-deposit product, you will not be able to access your funds for the duration of the loan. However, if you have subscribed to one of these products, but you really need funds, you can transfer a portion of these in flexible deposits.

The subscription to fixed-proof products takes place in specific amounts called lots. Each lot represents a fixed amount of cryptocurrency that will accumulate interest based on a predefined rate. Also, to prevent a few large holders from buying the entire pool, there is an individual limit for each account on the number of lots that you can buy.

Generally, the loan period is 14 or 30 days. On the subscription day, Binance lending takes funds from your Exchange Wallet and adds them to your lending wallet.

For fixed deposits, you will see the following information on.

- Annualized Interest Rate. This is the percentage return you will receive if you subscribe to this product for 12 months.
- Duration. This is the duration for which your funds will be frozen and will earn interest.
- Lot Size. This is the amount of crypto contained in a lot. For example, 1 lot = 100 BUSD.
- Maximum Quantity. This is the maximum amount that an individual account can buy.
- Subscription Begins. This is the date you can start subscribing funds to this product.
- Subscription Expires. This is the date on which the subscription period ends. Note that the subscription period may end before this date in case the maximum limit is reached.
- Value Date. This is the date your funds start to accumulate interest.
- Redemption Date. This is the date your funds are released, and interest is paid.

## Flexible deposits

Flexible deposits are essentially your crypto savings account. They have lower interest rates than Fixed Deposits.

It is important to note that when you subscribe your funds to a flexible deposit product, they are blocked for that day. This means that they will not accumulate interest, and you will not be able to withdraw them until the following day. From the day following your subscription, your funds will be unlocked, earn interest and be redeemable at any time. These measures prevent the system from being fooled.

When redeeming funds, you can choose between standard or quick refund. When you choose the fast repayment, your funds will be available immediately, but you will not receive the accumulated interest on that day. If, on the other hand, you choose the standard refund, your funds will be released the following day, and you will also receive interest on the day you requested the refund.

The interest of flexible products is distributed every day. Flexible deposit products are closed for subscription from 23:50 to 00:10 UTC. Subscription rates are reset during this interval.

We have tried both options and we have made some decent returns on our investments. We recommend you fixed deposits if you plan to hold your coins for a very long time.

# Chapter 11 - Crypto and Passive Income: Binance Dual Savings

Binance offers several practical ways to earn passive income, but they may expose you to price risk. The ability to use more volatile cryptocurrencies to generate income is attractive, but these are directly related to market conditions.

You can also use stablecoins, such as BUSD or USDT, but Binance Dual Savings takes this concept to the next level. You have the opportunity to receive returns regardless of the direction of the market. Let's see how it works.

## What is Binance Dual Savings?

Binance Dual Savings allows you to deposit one cryptocurrency and earn on the basis of two assets. Commit your crypto funds, block a specific interest rate, but earn more if the value of the committed funds increases. Basically it's a way to have more control over your risk.

The return received depends on the outcome of your bet on the expiry date. If the value of your funds increases as long as your earnings exceed the savings rate, you will get a higher return. If the value of your funds does not exceed the savings rate, you will still receive the return on the funds you have blocked.

Before we delve into how these products work, let's explain some of the terms you will need to know.

- Subscription Deadline. This is the date that ends the period in which to commit funds to this Dual Savings product.
- Expiry date. This is the day you can redeem your crypto with the interest earned.
- Strike Price. This is the price limit that determines in which currency you will receive the payment.
- Settlement Price. This is the price of your cryptocurrencies on the expiration date. It is calculated using an index composed of the most liquid BTC-USD spot trading pairs on the market.
- Rate of Return. This is the fixed interest you will receive upon settlement of the product.
- Annualized Rate of Return. This is the interest you would earn by locking your crypto into a Dual Savings product for one year. For example, if your annualized rate of return is 365%, your estimated daily return will be 1%.

## Dual Savings work on BTC

The Dual Savings product on BTC allows BTC holders to hedge their funds in Bitcoin.

The idea is that if the settlement price is higher than the strike price, the product is settled in BUSD. Conversely, if the settlement price is lower than the strike price, the product is settled in BTC.

This means that if the product is settled in BUSD, you can actually sell your BTC at a price higher than the spot price at the time of expiration.

So how are interest rates calculated for this product? The higher the strike price and the shorter the period, the lower the yield. The lower the strike price and the longer the period, the higher the yield.

Let's make an example. Suppose you have 1 BTC at a price of $10,000, and you subscribe to a 30-day Dual Savings product with a 2% rate of return. The strike price is set at $ 12,000.

After 30 days, one of these two possibilities will happen.

- If BTC is over $12,000, your 1 BTC is paid in 12,000 BUSD plus 2% of interest of 240 BUSD. Now you have 12.240 BUSD.

- If BTC is under $ 12,000, you will receive back your 1 BTC and 2% of interest of 0.02 BTC. Now you have 1.02 BTC.

## Dual Savings work BUSD / USDT

StableCoin-based Dual Savings products allow you to actually buy BTC at a lower price than the current spot price at the time of maturity.

Suppose you have 10,000 BUSD when the price of 1 BTC is $10,000. You subscribe to a 30-day Dual Savings product with a 2% return rate. The exercise price is set at $8,000.

After 30 days, one of these two possibilities will occur:

- If BTC is above $8,000, you receive your 10,000 BUSD back together with the interest of 2% of 200 BUSD. Now you have 10,200 BUSD.
- If BTC is $ 8,000, your 10,000 BUSD are paid as 1 BTC over 2% of interest of 0.02 BTC. Now you have 1.02 BTC.

This model is incredibly interesting and we have used it a couple of times. We encourage you to check it out.

# Chapter 12 - Other Ways to Earn Passive Income with Your Crypto

Trading or investing in projects is one of the ways to make money in the blockchain industry. However, these typically require detailed research and a substantial investment of time. Furthermore, they do not guarantee a reliable source of income.

Even the best investors can find themselves in prolonged periods of loss, and one of the ways to survive is to have alternative sources of income.

There are other methods besides trading or investing that can help you increase your cryptocurrency funds. These can generate a steady income similar to interest, but require little setup effort and no maintenance effort.

In this way, you can have different streams of income which, combined with each other, can reach a significant amount. Let's take a look at some ways to earn passive income on your crypto.

## Mining

Mining is essentially about using computational power to protect a network in order to receive a reward. While it does not require you to have cryptocurrency funds, it is the oldest method of earning passive income in the crypto field.

In the early days of Bitcoin, mining on an everyday Central Processing Unit (CPU) was a viable solution. As the network hash rate increased, most miners switched to using powerful Graphics Processing Units (GPUs). As competition escalates, mining has become an almost exclusive playground for Application-Specific Integrated Circuits (ASICs). These are devices that use mining chips tailored for this specific purpose.

The ASIC industry is highly competitive and dominated by corporations with significant resources available for research and development. By the time these chips hit the retail market, they are likely already obsolete and require a considerable amount of mining time to cover the purchase costs.

As a result, Bitcoin mining has become a corporate business rather than a viable source of passive income for the average individual.

On the other hand, mining Proof of Work coins with a lower hash rate can still be a profitable business for some. On these networks, it is still possible to use GPUs. Mining lesser-known coins brings with it a higher potential reward, but also greater risk. Mined coins can lose all their value overnight, have low liquidity, have bugs, or be damaged by many other factors.

It is important to note that setting up and maintaining mining equipment requires an initial investment and some technical skills.

## Staking

Staking is essentially a less demanding alternative to mining. It typically involves holding funds in a suitable wallet and performing various functions on the network (such as validating transactions) to receive staking rewards. Staking incentivizes the maintenance of network security through ownership.

Usually, staking involves setting up a wallet for this activity. Once you have done it, you simply need to store the coins in it to earn rewards. In some cases, the process involves adding or delegating funds to a staking pool. Some exchanges do this on your behalf. All you have to do is keep your tokens on the exchange and the platform will take care of all the technical requirements.

Staking can be a great way to increase your cryptocurrency funds with minimal effort. However, some staking projects use tactics to artificially inflate estimates of profit rates generated by staking. It is essential to analyze the economic models of tokens as they can greatly influence the estimates on staking rewards.

## Lending

Lending is a completely passive way to earn interest on your cryptocurrency funds. There are several peer-to-peer lending platforms that allow you to store your funds over a period of time and collect interest payments when it expires. The interest rate can be fixed or based on the current market rate.

Some exchanges that offer margin trading have this feature implemented on their platform.

This method is ideal for long-term investors who want to increase their funds with little effort. It is important to underline that blocking funds in a smart contract carries the risk of bugs.

## Managing a Lightning node

The Lightning Network is a second layer protocol that operates on top of a blockchain, such as Bitcoin. It is an off-chain micropayment network, which means it can be used for fast transactions that are not immediately transferred to the underlying blockchain.

Typical transactions on the Bitcoin network are one-way. Therefore, if Alice sends a bitcoin to Bob, Bob cannot use the same payment channel to send that coin back to Alice. The

Lightning Network, on the other hand, uses two-way channels that require the two participants to agree on the terms of the transaction in advance.

Lightning nodes provide liquidity and increase the capacity of the Lightning Network by blocking bitcoins in payment channels. They then collect commissions from payments that go through their channels.

Running a Lightning node can be tricky for non-technical bitcoin investors, and the rewards depend heavily on the overall Lightning Network adoption.

## Affiliate programs

Some crypto companies reward you for bringing new users to their platform. These include affiliate links, referrals or some other type of discount offered to new users introduced by you to the platform.

If you have a large social media audience, affiliate programs can be a great way to earn extra income. However, it is always important to research the services in advance so as not to spread the word about low quality projects.

## Masternodes

Simply put, a masternode is similar to a server but runs on a decentralized network and has functionality that other nodes in the network do not have.

Token projects tend to grant special privileges to actors who have a strong incentive to maintain network stability. Masternodes require a substantial initial investment and considerable technical expertise to set up.

For some masternodes, the token balance requirement can be so high that the pool is illiquid. Projects with masternodes also tend to inflate estimated income rates, so the Do Your Own Research (DYOR) principle is always essential before investing in one of them.

## Forks and airdrops

Taking advantage of a hard fork is a relatively simple tactic for investors. It only requires you to have the forked coins at the time of the hard fork. If there are two or more competing chains after the fork, the investor will have a token balance for each.

Airdrops are similar to forks in that they only require you to have a wallet address at the time of the airdrop. Some exchanges distribute airdrops to their users. Remember that receiving an airdrop will never require you to share your private keys. If you are asked for them, it is an obvious sign of a scam.

## Blockchain-based content creation platforms

The advent of distributed ledger technologies have allowed the creation of new types of content platforms. These allow creators to monetize their content in several unique ways and without the inclusion of annoying advertisements.

In such a system, content creators retain ownership of their creations and usually monetize attention in some way. This can take a lot of work initially but can provide a stable source of income once a substantial content set is ready.

## Potential risks

Here are some risks associated with all these methods.

- Buying a low-quality asset. Inflated or misleading income rates can lure investors into buying an asset that would otherwise have a very low value. Some staking networks adopt a multi-token system where the rewards are distributed in a second token, which creates a constant selling pressure for the reward token.

- User mistakes. As the blockchain industry is still in its infancy, setting up and maintaining these sources of income requires technical skills and an investigative mindset. For some holders, it may be best to wait for these services to become user-friendly, or use only those that require minimal technical expertise.

- Blocking periods. Some lending or staking methods require you to block your funds for a certain period of time. This makes your funds illiquid for that range, leaving you vulnerable to any event that could negatively affect the asset's price.

- Bugs. Locking your tokens in a staking wallet or smart contract always carries the risk of bugs. Typically, there are several choices available with varying degrees of quality. It is essential to research these options before using one. Open source software could be a good place to start as these options are at least controlled by the community.

We encourage you to experiment with these different forms of passive income. However, never risk more than you can afford to lose and do your own research before putting your capital at risk.

# Chapter 13 - Hyperinflation and Cryptocurrency

We want to dedicate the last chapter of this book to why we believe the world of cryptocurrency is going to revolutionize the financial system as we know it. We believe that hyperinflation for the US Dollar is right around the corner, considering how much money printing the FED has been doing since early 2020.

First of all, let's try to understand what hyperinflation is.

All economies have a certain degree of inflation, which occurs when the average price of goods increases, while the purchasing power of money decreases. Typically, governments and financial institutions work together to ensure that inflation occurs gradually and smoothly. However, history has many instances where the rate of inflation has accelerated to an unprecedented level, causing the national currency to drop significantly in alarming proportions. This accelerated rate of inflation is what we call hyperinflation.

In his book, "The Monetary Dynamics of Hyperinflation," economist Philip Cagan states that periods of hyperinflation begin when the price of goods and services increases by more than 50% within a month. For example, if the price of a pack of rice goes from $10 to $15 in less than 30 days, and from $15 to $22.50 by the end of the following month, we would have hyperinflation. If this trend continues, the price for the same pack of rice could reach $114 in six months, and over $1,000 in a year.

It is rare for the hyperinflation rate to remain stable at 50%. In most cases, these rates accelerate so rapidly that the price of various goods and services can drastically increase in a single day or even a few hours. Due to rising prices, consumer confidence decreases and the value of the country's currency collapses. Eventually, hyperinflation causes a chain reaction that leads to bankruptcies, increased unemployment and reduced tax revenues. Renowned episodes of hyperinflation have occurred in Germany, Venezuela and Zimbabwe, but several other countries have experienced a similar crisis, including Hungary, Yugoslavia, Greece and many others.

## Hyperinflation in Germany

One of the most famous examples of hyperinflation occurred in Germany, in the Weimar Republic after the First World War. Germany had borrowed huge amounts of money to finance the war effort, convinced that it could win the war and use the reparations to pay off debts. Not only did they end up losing the war, but the Germans had to pay billions of dollars in repairs.

Despite debates over the causes of hyperinflation in Germany, some causes that are often cited include the suspension of the gold standard, war reparations and the reckless issuance of banknotes. The decision to suspend the gold standard at the start of the conflict meant that the amount of money in circulation did not correspond to the value of the gold owned by the nation. This controversial development led to the devaluation of the German currency, forcing the victors of the World War to demand reparations in any currency other than the German marks. Germany reacted by printing huge quantities of its own currency to buy foreign currencies, causing a further collapse.

At some stages during this episode, the inflation rate was increasing by more than 20% per day. The German currency became so useless that someone burned the banknotes to heat the house, as they cost less than wood.

## Hyperinflation in Venezuela

Thanks to its large oil reserves, Venezuela maintained a regular economy during the 20th century. However, the oil glut in the 1980s, followed by economic mismanagement and corruption in the early 21st century, led to a major socioeconomic and political crisis. The crisis started in 2010 and is currently considered one of the worst in history.

The inflation rate in Venezuela has increased rapidly, from an annual rate of 69% in 2014 to 181% in 2015. The period of hyperinflation began in 2016, marked by an inflation of 800% by the end of the year. It was followed by 4,000% in 2017 and over 2,600,000% in early 2019.

In 2018, President Nicolás Maduro announced the issuance of a new currency to combat hyperinflation, replacing the existing bolivar at a rate of 1 / 100,000. Hence, 100,000 bolivars were converted into 1 sovereign bolivar. However, the effectiveness of such an approach is highly questionable. Economist Steve Hanke said that eliminating zeroes has only an "aesthetic function".

## Hyperinflation in Zimbabwe

In the first years after the country's independence in 1980, Zimbabwe's economy was fairly stable. However, in 1991 the government of President Robert Mugabe initiated a program called the Economic Structural Adjustment Program (ESAP), which is considered the primary cause of the country's economic collapse. In addition to the ESAP, a redistribution of land carried out by the authorities has resulted in a drastic reduction in food production, leading to a serious financial and social crisis.

The Zimbabwean dollar began to show signs of instability in the late 1990s, and episodes of hyperinflation began in the early 2000s. The annual inflation rate reached 624% in 2004, 1,730% in 2006 and 231,150,888% in July. 2008. Due to the lack of data provided by the country's central bank, rates after this month are based on theoretical estimates.

According to the calculations of Professor Steve H. Hanke, hyperinflation in Zimbabwe peaked in November 2008, with an annual rate of 89.7 sextillion percent, equivalent to 79.6 billion percent per month, or 98% per day.

Zimbabwe was the first country to experience hyperinflation in the 21st century, recording the second worst episode of inflation in history. In 2008, the ZWN was officially abandoned, adopting foreign currencies as legal tender.

## The use of cryptocurrencies

Since Bitcoin and other cryptocurrencies are not based on centralized systems, their value cannot be determined by financial or government institutions. Blockchain technology ensures that the issuance of new units follows a predefined schedule and that each of them is unique and immune to duplication. These are some of the reasons why cryptocurrencies are becoming increasingly popular, especially in countries struggling with hyperinflation, such as Venezuela.

Similar cases are also observed in Zimbabwe, where peer-to-peer digital currencies have seen a notable increase in use cases. In some countries, authorities are examining the possibilities and risks associated with introducing a government-backed cryptocurrency as a potential alternative to the traditional fiat currency system. The Swedish central bank is among the first in this field. Other examples of this include the central banks of Singapore, Canada, China and the US.

Although episodes of hyperinflation may seem few and far between, it is clear that a relatively short period of political or social tensions can quickly lead to the devaluation of traditional currencies. A lower demand for a single country's export may be a cause. Once the currency loses value, prices rise very quickly, creating a vicious circle. Several governments have tried to tackle the problem by printing new money, but this tactic proved useless and only contributed to the further decrease in the overall value. It is interesting to note that when confidence in traditional currency decreases, that in cryptocurrencies tends to increase. This could have strong implications for the future of the concept of money globally.

We believe that when hyperinflation will come to first world countries. Bitcoin and other cryptocurrency are going to skyrocket. We are holding up to that point and then we will hold even more.

We never sell our crypto. Diamond hands.

# Conclusion

Congratulations on making it to the end of this book, we hope you found some useful insights to take your cryptocurrency trading skills to the next level. As you should know by now, the world of cryptocurrency is extremely complicated and there is a new "opportunity" every way you look. However, our experience tells us that only by taking things seriously and having a proper plan you can develop your investing skills to the point that you can actually accumulate wealth.

Our final advice is to stay away from the shining objects that the world of cryptocurrencies offers you every day. Simply study the world of cryptocurrencies in depth and when you feel ready try to invest a little bit of money. Analyze your results, improve your money management skills and become the master of your emotions.

As you can see, there are no shortcuts you can take. Easy money does not exist. What exists is the possibility to start from zero and work your way up to become a professional cryptocurrency investor. The journey might be difficult, but it is certainly worth it.

To your success!